Markets and
Minorities

Markets and Minorities

THOMAS SOWELL

Basic Books, Inc., Publishers   New York

This book has been sponsored by The International Center
for Economic Policy Studies

First published in the United States by Basic Books, Inc., New York,
1981
Copyright © 1981 by The International Center for Economic Policy
Studies

Library of Congress Catalog Number: 81–66107
ISBN: 0–465–04398–4 (cloth)
ISBN: 0–465–04399–2 (paper)

Printed in the United States of America
10 9 8 7 6 5 4 3 2 1

Contents

Foreword

Milton Friedman

This book is a breath of fresh air on a topic that, more than most others, is generally the subject of unreasoning passion, emotion, and prejudice.

The breath of fresh air is driven by passion — by the deep and sincere passion of a remarkable man — but the passion is disciplined by reason, by intellectual integrity, and by the careful and intelligent examination of a wide range of evidence. Few scholars have ranged so widely as Thomas Sowell over the historical and quantitative evidence on the conditions of minorities, even fewer have had the logical ability and command of economic analysis to extract from that evidence its fundamental implications, and fewer still have combined these characteristics with the expository skill that enables Sowell to convey his findings to any interested reader, regardless of that reader's technical training.

I can speak from personal experience about the passion — both its depth and sincerity. When Thomas Sowell completed his work for the doctorate in economics at the University of Chicago (itself a remarkable achievement, given his background as described so well in his partly autobiographical book, *Black Education: Myths and Tragedies*[David McKay, c. 1972]), he received a number of attractive offers of teaching positions — as was to be expected for one of our outstanding students. He talked to several of us about which to accept, expressing a strong preference for accepting one of the least attractive offers — at Howard University in Washington — on the purely emotional ground that it would enable him to make the greatest contribution to the improvement of members of his race. I tried to dissuade him — as did others of my colleagues. I urged on him that he would do far more for blacks by demonstrating that he could compete successfully in the largely white scholarly world as a whole than by teaching at a predominantly black institution which was less renowned in scholarship and research than other institutions from which he had offers.

Despite all the advice, Tom insisted on going to Howard. A few months later, a telephone call came from him asking if it was consistent with academic ethics to resign in the middle of a semester — the occasion being attempts by administrators to interfere with his teaching. When I replied in the negative, he asked whether alteration of the grades he assigned to students by an academic superior would change the situation. I said it would. As it happened, interference with his teaching did not go to that extreme, so he stuck it out to the end of the academic year, and then resigned.

This episode encapsulates some of the qualities — beyond his deep concern for the disadvantaged of all races — that have made Thomas Sowell such an outstanding person and scholar and that make this such a fine and important book. First, stubbornness — at once exasperating when he disagrees with you and yet fundamental to his scholarly achievements. He has a mind of his own, insists on making it up for himself, and on getting the evidence necessary to form a valid judgment. This quality — which we call persistence in ourselves, stubbornness in someone we are fond of, obstinacy in still others — explains the extraordinary range of evidence he has assembled in the whole series of books and articles that he has written on the subject of minorities.

Second, an open mind, a readiness to alter his views, but only on the basis of evidence and argument. He respects the opinion of others, not as the final word, but as guiding his own selection and examination of evidence.

Third, intellectual integrity, an insistence on high standards both for himself and for his students, whatever the color of their skin — a trait that he has demonstrated over and over again in his career, sometimes at great personal cost.

Fourth, personal integrity, so that he has never been willing to sacrifice what he regarded as a basic principle for the sake of expediency or temporary advantage.

The reader of this book will find these qualities reflected on every page. He will find a distillation of many years of thorough and thoughtful work. He will learn not only about factors affecting the economic conditions of minorities, about the role of markets, non-market institutions, and government in altering those conditions, but also, and no less important, how to think about and understand such questions.

I have no doubt that this slim volume will become a classic in the literature on the economics and social problems of minorities.

Ely, Vermont
July 1980

Introduction

This book applies basic economic principles to the study of racial and ethnic minorities. It is intended for undergraduate economics students familiar with such elementary concepts as supply and demand curves, and profit-maximization conditions.

An economic framework is used throughout the book, even where the subject matter may appear to be sociological, historical, or political. By an economic framework is meant not only the use of particular economic concepts, but also the systematic application of cause-and-effect analysis, based upon the incentives and constraints actually facing various decision-makers — whether employers, landlords, or workers.

In applying the general logic of decision-making to particular social processes, we will examine the peculiarities of those processes but will treat human beings as similar, whether they are in politics or business or schools. We will not assume that public officials are a different breed of creatures, nor treat the government as a *deus ex machina*, operating without any of the ordinary motives of human beings. We will also avoid making "the market " an automatic producer of certain results, but will instead consider what kinds of markets are being analyzed, and what incentives and constraints exist in such markets. Nor will we engage in the fashionable practice of talking about what "society" has decided. The whole emphasis will be on the specific characteristics of particular decision-making processes — not on a vague figure of speech called "society".

Theories will be confronted with facts. Sometimes a less plausible theory will prove more consistent with the facts than a theory that seemed more reasonable at the outset. For example, the degree of racial residential integration in American cities was often far greater in the last quarter of the nineteenth century (when no real effort was made to achieve it) than in the last quarter of the twentieth century (after decades of political and legal struggles). This is difficult — if not impossible — to explain in terms of the more conventional theories of racial relations, but it fits other theories that have not enjoyed nearly as much popularity.

Many other intriguing results emerge when other beliefs are analyzed as hypotheses rather than repeated as creeds. However, the central aim of this book is not to assert or defend particular conclusions but to demonstrate the application of an analytical process. The reader can then use the same principles to investigate whatever he chooses and reach his own conclusions.

Thomas Sowell

CHAPTER ONE

The Application of Economics

While the economic conditions of racial and ethnic minorities are constantly discussed in the mass media, this is very different from saying that these discussions apply economic analysis to these questions. Applying the tools of the economic trade to public policy issues involving race or ethnically means, first of all, treating such matters as *cause-and-effect* questions about how things have come to be what they are, and about the likely consequences of alternative policies. If this is not to be a purely theoretical exericse, it must also include *empirical evidence* bearing on the correctness or incorrectness of alternative beliefs about the causal relationships involved.

Simple as this may seem, it goes counter to volumes of assertions, rhetoric, and moralizing over race and ethnicity in America. The application of economics means proceeding systematically by (1) defining the variables to be tested, (2) analytically deriving the implications of alternative theories of causation involving these variables, (3) confronting these implications with observable evidence to see which best fit the facts. In short, economic reasoning is a process of going from various overlapping, and to some extent contradictory, *beliefs* to a systematically constructed and internally consistent *theory*, from which specific *hypotheses* about observable events can be logically derived and then confronted with *evidence* — that is, facts which would be different if the theory were correct than if the theory were not correct.

A mere jumble of beliefs and facts is not theory or hypothesis-testing. It is possible to select — in retrospect — facts consistent with almost any belief. Systematic analysis deduces prospective conclusions which may or may not prove consistent with independently generated facts. Given the complexities of the real world and the limitations of the human mind, the choice is often not between 100 per cent right and 100 per cent wrong theories, but between theories which explain more of a phenomenon rather than less, or which explain a wider range of phenomena, or which explain given phenomena with fewer, simpler, or clearer assumptions.

Systematic procedures are necessary for testing alternative beliefs, because choosing on the basis of plausibility means perpetuating whatever respective intellectual or ideological predispositions we already have, which determine what each of us will find plausible, bringing us no nearer to a commonly acceptable conclusion among differently oriented people. Deliberation has been defined as losing our freedom (de-liberation) to choose to believe whatever we wish. It is not an externally imposed loss of freedom but a chosen relinquishing of a dangerous kind of freedom, which would leave us no way of settling differences other than shouting each other down, or, ultimately, fighting. These non-analytic methods are initially easier, and have in fact been tried to some extent in all multi-ethnic societies — usually leading to mutual frustration, sometimes to oppression or even extermination of some segment of the society, or even to the destruction of the society as a whole. In short, there are practical as well as intellectual reasons for systematic analysis.

Within the general framework of systematic analysis, economic analysis has its own specific concepts and theories, derived from a wide range of social phenomena, and applicable to particular questions, such as those concerning ethnicity. How correct these will prove to be in practice is an empirical question to be dealt with in the light of the facts to be found. But before proceeding to that, it will be necessary to distinguish a theory's *axioms* from its *hypotheses*, because these are frequently confused in discussions of ethnic groups and their economic conditions.

Axioms simply assert — without evidence or proof — that certain relationships are true: "the shortest distance between two points is a straight line", or "things equal to the same thing are equal to each other". Most of the enduring axioms are either self-evident or at least things which no one has ever challenged, or challenged successfully. This may be either because they are true or because of difficulties in formulating them in terms that would permit a real test. Axioms are a part of a theory which are not intended to be tested, though the theory as a whole may be tested and found to be "right" or "wrong" — or, more precisely, better or worse than some alternative theory. Hypotheses — the specific conclusions derived from a general theory — are of course intended to be tested. Axioms exist because a theory has to start somewhere, and because we could debate every conception or relationship endlessly without ever reaching the point where an hypothesis could be tested. An axiom is an arbitrary device to get us started toward confronting the real issues.

Problems arise when people do not distinguish between axiomatic assertions and testable hypotheses. For example, which of the following statements about ethnic groups are hypotheses and which are axioms?

1 Ethnic minorities as a group are economically disadvantaged in the sense that they fall below the national average in income and occupational status.

2 Discrimination accounts for the difference between the incomes of ethnic minorities and the general population.

3 A non-random (disproportionate) representation of ethnic group members in high-level and low-level occupations, or in various institutions (jails, universities, etc.), measures the degree of discrimination.

4 Color differences constitute a unique economic disadvantage for those groups genetically, indelibly, and enduringly different from the general population.

5   The defeat of racism is essential to the economic and social
    advancement of racially distinct minorities.

6   Political power is the key to economic advancement.

   All of these are weighty considerations that will be dealt
with somewhere in this book. The point here is simply to see
whether they are axioms or hypotheses. The answer is that
they can be either. The problem is when what is arbitrarily
postulated as an axiom is later treated as if it were a testable
hypothesis or — worse yet — a proven fact. A deeply felt
conviction or a widely shared belief is not a verified
hypothesis. When axiomatic assertions become the basis for
either predictions or public policy, the results can be far from
what was expected. Hypotheses are verified for a reason.

ECONOMIC ANALYSIS

Economics has its own axioms, hypotheses, and procedures.
The great variety of circumstances in which these are applied
can be summarized as market transactions and non-market
transactions. This traditional terminology may be somewhat
vague, or even misleading.
   By "market" transactions are meant such transactions as
are voluntarily made on terms chosen or negotiated by the
transacting parties themselves. The "market", as it is called,
need not exist anywhere in time or space. Far from being a
particular set of institutions, it is simply the freedom to
choose among options and institutions that may be available,
or to create them to suit the needs or desires of the transacting
parties. To get one's food "through the market" can mean
anything from buying groceries in a supermarket to eating in
restaurants, or being fed in exchange for work or sex. It is the
set of prospective options rather than the actual
retrospectively observed choice which defines "the market".
Non-market transactions are those in which the transactors
alone do not determine the options to select or the terms of
their transactions. That is, external agencies — cartels,
unions, government — constrain or even direct their choices.
Economists often call this "intervention" in "the market", as if

it were an act taking place at a particular location, rather than a prospective threat of sanctions constraining the choice process in people's minds.

While it is useful to dichotomize actual transactions into "market" and non-market, it is also necessary to realize that the real world seldom fits any definition perfectly. Taken to its literal extreme, market choices made solely by the transactors would mean that no one else would be involved, whether or not they lived up to their agreements or robbed, cheated, or killed each other. In such a world, transactions costs would be so high that few, if any, transactions could take place. To keep transactions costs within some reasonable limits, it is necessary to have a whole framework of laws and organized force (government) behind such laws. Thus, market transactions in practice are distinguished from non-market transactions by whether external agencies simply reserve sanctions to enforce terms chosen by the transactors or whether the external agencies constrain or choose the terms themselves.

Ethnic minority individuals or groups may seek their goals through market or non-market processes, like everyone else. The economic question is: What are the consequences of these different processes, for them and for the larger society? This involves both the cause-and-effect question of predicting results and the normative question of determining what results are preferable.

In attempting to determine cause and effect, economic theory includes both (1) individual or *intentional* motivation, and (2) *systemic* relationships which may bring about results not intended by any of the agents involved. There are many examples of this distinction in various fields. Intricate ecological patterns may emerge among different species of trees, bushes, insects, and animals without any of these organisms having intended any such results. Darwin argued that man himself could evolve without any intentional supernatural design, such as those postulated by earlier religious philosophers. [1] According to the Marxian theory of history, "what each individual wills is obstructed by everyone else, and what emerges is something that no one willed". [2] Modern students of economics are of course aware of the Keynesian proposition that when everyone decides to save more, the result can be *less* total saving.

The distinction between intentional motivation and systemic effects is particularly important in dealing with economic questions involving ethnic groups. It is often taken as axiomatic that adverse intentions (racism, prejudice) are solely responsible for adverse results. An economic analysis must treat this as a testable hypothesis. It must determine as best it can to what extent intentional or systemic factors account for observed conditions.

Economic theory may be complete when it has determined cause-and-effect relationships and verified them with factual evidence. Economic policy, however, must then determine which of the available alternatives is preferable. On this there is no scientific answer or scientific way to reach an answer. What is preferable to A is not preferable to B, and the economist has no special mandate to impose his own personal preferences, either openly or hidden in his policy recommendations. Economic tradition has evolved the concept of "optimality" (or "Pareto optimality", after its originator) to deal with this impasse. A situation is said to be "optimal" if there are no transfers remaining to be made among the people involved that could make any of them better off — according to their own respective preferences — without making others worse off by their respective preferences. One of the ways of judging economic policy for minorities is whether it fulfills this condition. There may, of course, be alternative criteria, such as whether a given policy benefits minorities, *regardless* of the nature or degree of its effect on others. Some policies would meet the criterion of Pareto optimality, while others would meet only the more limited criterion of helping minorities at indefinite costs to others, and still other policies might meet neither or both criteria. What is necessary for our purposes is only to be explicitly aware of which standard is being applied in a particular instance.

The traditional economic conception of optimality is morally neutral. It treats individual preferences as parameters, which logically determine what results would be optimal under specified conditions. It does not provide "better" preferences or beliefs for those whose behavior it analyzes. Moreover, it is not always true that market equilibrium will coincide with Pareto optimality. Where the parties affected by economic decisions are not identical with the parties making (or influencing) the decision, then transactions may be made that are optimal for the transactors, but with costly effects on third parties. Water and air pollution are classic examples, though by no means the sole examples.

Among the axioms of economics that will be incorporated into the analysis are the propositions that (1) more of any given good or attribute will be acquired when the price is lower, (2) more of any given good or attribute will be supplied when the price is higher, (3) more income is preferred to less, whenever other sacrifices need not be made to get it, and (4) transactors either have or can acquire knowledge of offers and bids, whenever the benefits exceed the costs — both as judged by the transactors. No attempt will be made here to prove these propositions, which are adopted as axioms from economics in general to be applied to the economics of ethnic groups. If they or any of the other elements of the economic analysis used are incorrect, that should become apparent when the resulting hypotheses are tested against the evidence. Moreover, alternative theories will be considered which do not incorporate these axioms.

SOME PRELIMINARY EVIDENCE

Humorist Will Rogers once said that it is not ignorance that hurts us, but all the things we know "that ain't so". Perhaps the most pervasive conception of American ethnic groups is that they are people who are quite different — economically, at least — from the national average, and different specifically in being worse off. This can, of course, be made *definitionally* true by counting as "minorities" only such ethnic groups as fall below the national average in income. But those who regard the proposition as a testable hypothesis — indeed a proven fact — do not mean it in this trivial, circular sense. Taking the proposition as intended, as a testable hypothesis, we can make some preliminary estimate of the extent to which it is true by comparing the incomes of various ethnic groups as a percentage of the income of the US population as a whole (see table 1.1).

Table 1.1   Family income by ethnic group

Ethnicity	Relative income (per cent of national average)
Jewish	172
Japanese	132
Polish	115
Chinese	112
Italian	112
German	107
Irish	102
Filipino	99
West Indian	94
Mexican	76
Puerto Rican	63
Black	62
American Indian	60

Sources: US Bureau of the Census and National Jewish Population Study. [3]

Clearly, there are American ethnic groups with incomes substantially above the national average, as well as substantially below it. The same result would be found if occupational status were substituted for income. Moreover, the supposedly pace-setting white Anglo-Saxon Protestants (WASPs) would have been also-rans if they had been included, their average income being 105 per cent of the national average. These results falsify the first four of the six propositions reviewed above, which may have seemed so obvious as to be axiomatic. Some of these propositions may be salvageable with appropriate restrictions, but that is itself a testable hypothesis rather than an axiomatic truth. Later chapters will attempt to determine to what extent they may be true in a modified sense. For now, it may be useful to review the ways in which the data falsify the hypotheses as presented:

1 Ethnic minorities' incomes differ so widely among themselves, ranging on both sides of the national average, as to call into question the meaningfulness of the national average itself — which is simply a statistical amalgamation of highly disparate income data, rather than a statement of what "most" Americans earn.

2 Discrimination clearly cannot account for the incomes of minorities who earn *more* than the national average, since those groups have neither the size nor the control necessary to discriminate against the general population. Nor can discrimination account for other ethnic groups' incomes being at the national average. It might account for minority incomes below the national average, but even that conclusion is less secure than it might be, given that there are vast other variations shown which are obviously explained by factors *other* than discrimination, and there is no *a priori* reason to arbitrarily exclude those other factors from any influence on the lower income groups.

3 Disproportionate over-representation of some ethnic minorities in high-level occupations clearly cannot be explained by discrimination — either by their discrimination against the general population or by the disappearance of all discrimination against them, since there is still independent evidence of continuing discrimination. Parallel to the reasoning pertaining to income, if disproportionate over-representation is explained by other factors than discrimination in these cases, it would be arbitrary to exclude those other factors from any possible influence on the under-representation of other groups. Again, as in the case of income, the "national average" or "representation" of various occupational levels is itself a statistical artifact — an amalgamation of wide-ranging group differences rather than a statement of a norm in any other sense.

4 Genetic color differences have not kept Orientals from having higher incomes than the average American nor black West Indians from having incomes that are comparable (94 per cent of the national average), nor has a white complexion spared Puerto Ricans from low incomes.

The point here is not to claim that there is no element of validity behind any of the propositions being tested. They will in fact be subjected to more detailed scrutiny in the chapters that follow. The point here is to demonstrate that plausibility is deceptive, and that even the most commonly accepted beliefs and convictions need testing — perhaps *especially* such beliefs and convictions.

Not only is it necessary to test variables commonly thought of as decisive determinants. It is also necessary to consider other variables which may not have attracted comparable attention. Particularly likely to be overlooked are systemic variables — variables not designed or intended by anybody to be what they are, but which may nevertheless affect the economic (and other) phenomena we are trying to explain. Among the systemic variables that need to be considered as regards American ethnic groups are (1) age, (2) geographic distribution, and (3) fertility rates.

Age
Ethnic groups differ greatly in median age, and age in turn influences income. The age differences can be seen in table 1.2.

Perhaps the simplest way to illustrate the great impact of age on income is to point out that differences in income between age groups are even greater than racial differences in income. Families headed by persons in the 45-54 year-old bracket averaged 93 per cent higher income than families headed by persons under 25 years of age in 1974, while white incomes the same year averaged 62 per cent higher than black incomes.[4]

With intergroup age differences running into decades — more than a quarter of a century between Hispanics and Jews — gross economic comparisons of ethnic groups are completely misleading. People of very different ages (i.e.

very different amounts of work experience) earn very different incomes, even when there are no ethnic differences. Therefore, differences between whole groups with different amounts of experience cannot be arbitrarily attributed to their differing ethnicity. This is especially true when comparing the statistical "representation" of various groups in high level occupations requiring many years of experience and/or education.

Table 1.2   Median age by ethnic group

Ethnicity	Median age
Jewish	46
Polish	40
Irish	37
Italian	36
German	36
Japanese	32
Total US	28
Chinese	27
Black	22
American Indian	20
Mexican	18
Puerto Rican	18

Source: US Bureau of the Census.[5]

Differences in median age are only part of the statistical picture. Because the highest incomes are generally reached in the 40s and 50s, the percentage of each ethnic group that is in these age brackets has an important weight in determining what the group's average income is. For example, just over half of the Jewish population of the United States is 45 years old or older, whle only 12 per cent of the Puerto Rican population is that old.[6]

Age is also important in a very different sense. American attitudes and policies toward racial or ethnic minorities are also changing.[7] This means that older members of low-income ethnic groups are likely to be particularly far behind their age-peers in the general population in both education and qualifying work experience. Their current incomes reflect past conditions — within their group and in the general society. Among the important consequences of this are:

1 Higher age-bracket members of low-income groups are likely to have lower incomes relative to their age-peers in the general population than do the younger members of the same group relative to their contemporaries in the society at large.

2 The current effects of current policy are found in the incomes and occupations of younger members of ethnic minorities, and only to a lesser extent in the incomes and occupations of minority group members who are older.

In short, age-cohort comparisons of ethnic groups can present both a different picture and a truer picture of current ethnic progress. For example, blacks over 45 years of age earn less than 60 per cent of the income of their age-peers in the general population, while blacks aged 18-24 earn 83 per cent of the income of their age-peers. The percentages are virtually the same for American Indians.[8] Puerto Ricans aged 18-24 earn 3 per cent *more* than their age-peers, but Puerto Ricans 65 and older earn 35 per cent *less*.[9]

Some rough indication of changing job qualification levels over time may be obtained by comparing the differing amounts of schooling achieved by differing age-cohorts within a given ethnic group. For example, half of all Mexican Americans aged 65 and older have less than five years of schooling, while that is true of only 7 per cent of the 25-29 year-old Mexican Americans. The data for Puerto Ricans is very similar, and the data for blacks are not very different.[10] Older Americans in general tend to have less education, but not with such extreme differences between age brackets.

The combination of demographic and educational characteristics throws light on the issue of inferring employer discrimination from "under-representation" in high-level occupations. Given that high level jobs typically require both experience and education, the current "under-representation" of low-income minorities in them is neither surprising nor proof of job discrimination. Those members of such groups who are old enough to have enough experience are particularly likely to lack the education. This does not disprove the existence of employer discrimination. It merely invalidates the use of "representation" percentages as a means of demonstrating or measuring it. Employment discrimination is a large subject in its own right, and will be analyzed more extensively in chapters 2 and 3.

Geographic Distribution

American ethnic groups are distributed geographically in patterns that differ greatly from one group to another. For example, Puerto Ricans are almost non-existent in those southwestern states where Mexican Americans are concentrated and half the black population is located in the South where Japanese, Italian, or Polish people seldom settled.

The economic significance of these varying geographical distribution patterns may be indicated by the fact that the median family income in California is 71 per cent higher than in Arkansas, and the median family income in Alaska is more than double what it is in Mississippi.[11] Gross statistics on ethnic income differences include substantial regional differences. For example, Mexican Americans and Puerto Ricans earn more than blacks nationally (see table 1.1 above), but blacks *outside the South* earn more than either of these Hispanic groups.[12] In short, the income advantage of these two Hispanic groups is neither racial nor ethnic, but locational.

The same ethnic group often earns radically different amounts in different places, just as the general population does. American Indians living in Chicago, New York, or Detroit earn more than twice as much as Indians living on reservations.[13] Mexican Americans living in the Detroit metropolitan area average more than double the income of Mexican Americans in the metropolitan areas of Laredo or Brownsville, Texas.

Rural-urban differences compound the regional and inter-city income differences. Partly these differences reflect differences in the local economies, but they can also reflect substantial differences in the social characteristics of the people themselves. For example, blacks in the north average about 10 points higher IQ than blacks in the South, and American Indians in the rural mid-west average two more children per married woman (aged 35-44) than among Indians in the urban north-east.[14] Social differences of this magnitude suggest that other, less quantifiable, differences also exist within the same ethnic group, and influence economic outcomes. Other data in later chapters bear this out.

How the various groups came to be distributed as they are is a fascinating study in economic history. During the era of wind-driven ships, when ocean voyages were long and unpredictable (one to three months), the bulk of the immigration to America originated in northern and western Europe. This was because most working people could not afford the cost of a transatlantic voyage on a passenger ship, and came over in the holds of cargo vessels. This in turn meant that they did not choose their destination in America, but landed wherever the ship was docking for commercial purposes. The established trade routes thereby predetermined the port of debarkation of immigrants from each part of Europe. Groups who arrived penniless, such as the Irish (and in a later era the Jews and Italians) tended to settle in the ports of debarkation. Others who arrived with enough money left for travel in the United States — such as the Germans and Scandinavians — chose their own destinations within the United States, often further inland.

The introduction of steamships making transatlantic voyages radically changed the ethnic composition of the emigration to America. Now people from southern and eastern Europe for the first time had access to the United States on shorter, more predictable (ten-day) voyages that were within the financial range of working people who saved. By the late 1880s the bulk of immigrants to America were now southern and eastern Europeans, whereas emigration before had always been largely from north-western Europe.

Such domestic American economic activity as canal building drew some of the poorer Irish immigrants out of their port cities to earn a living doing this hard and dangerous work. After these transportation facilities were built, the Irish tended to settle down in communities along the routes of the canals and railroads they had built. Other groups became attached to other industries, and their economic and locational fate became likewise intertwined with the economic history of these industries.

Other groups have simply settled in those parts of the United States closest to their respective countries of origin — Orientals on the west coast, Cubans in Florida, and Mexicans in the south-west. The availability of air and shipping routes to the port of New York facilitated the settlement of West Indians and Puerto Ricans there. Blacks' destinations were first chosen by others who forcibly brought them to America, but it was not a random choice. They were concentrated in that region of the country whose climate and soil were favorable to the kind of crops that could be grown under the special conditions of slavery.[15]

Fertility Rates
Fertility rates vary greatly among ethnic groups, and these variations affect their economic well-being in many ways. For example, table 1.1 above shows Mexican American families earning significantly higher incomes than black families, but high fertility rates cause Mexican Americans to have lower *per capita* income than blacks.[16] Having "more mouths to feed" may be part of the reason why Mexican Americans live in substandard housing more so than blacks and send their children to college less often.[17]

The large intergroup differences in age (see table 1.2 above), which affect experience and income, are largely a function of differing fertility rates among ethnic minorities. More than half of all Mexican Americans and Puerto Ricans are either infants, children, or teenagers, as shown by their median age of 18. *Changes* in fertility rates over time also profoundly affect the age distribution of an ethnic group. Three groups have cut their fertility rates by more than half since 1910 — Jewish, Polish and Italian Americans[18] — and these are three of the four oldest groups in table 1.2. With large families the norm when their older generation was born, and much smaller families common when their younger generation was born, the disproportionate number of older people means a group average age considerably above the national average. Groups which still maintain a high fertility rate have correspondingly younger average ages.

Comparing women nearing completion of their childbearing years, table 1.3 shows the number of children per woman aged 35-44.

Table 1.3   Number of children by ethnic group

Ethnicity	Children per woman
American Indian	4.4
Mexican	4.4
Black	3.7
Puerto Rican	3.5
Irish	3.1
Filipino	3.0
Chinese	2.9
Polish	2.5
West Indian	2.5
Italian	2.4
Jewish	2.4
Japanese	2.2

Source: US Bureau of the Census. [19]

A generally inverse relationship between children and income can be seen by comparing table 1.3 with table 1.1. This inverse correlation is not perfect, but the four highest fertility groups are also the four lowest income groups, and the two lowest fertility groups are also the two highest income groups.

There are many reasons for the inverse relationship between children and income. Child bearing and child-tending reduces a woman's availability for employment and her ability to accumulate work experience or education, and it reduces both parents' mobility for seeking their best employment opportunities. There may also be different attitudes toward life in general between people who have many children and those who restrict their family size, and these attitudinal differences may also affect their work and their incomes.

One of the curious patterns found among low-income ethnic groups is that, while such groups generally have more children than average — and more children than equally poor members of the general population — the better educated or higher income portions of such ethnic groups have *fewer* children than equally well-educated or equally affluent members of the general population. For example, despite Mexican Americans' very high fertility rates, Mexican American wives with four years of high school have fewer children than the national average among similarly educated wives in the general population.[20] Similar patterns have been found in studies of fertility patterns among blacks, whose upper socio-economic classes have long had fertility rates too low to reproduce themselves.[21] There are grim economic implications in such fertility patterns. Much of the often painfully acquired "human capital" of the more fortunate segment of the group is lost when they die, because they do not leave an equal number of heirs to whom it could be passed on. The disadvantaged portions of the ethnic group produce more of the next generation in proportion to their numbers in the population. Therefore, much of the hard struggle upward from poverty has to be repeated from scratch, in each generation, rather than proceeding like a relay race in which the new generation could begin with the advantages achieved by those who went before them.

SUMMARY

The purpose of this book will be to systematically analyze the economic conditions of American ethnic groups in cause-and-effect terms. Many current beliefs about minorities do not survive intact from even a preliminary analysis of this sort. Variables commonly thought of as decisive — skin color, for example — prove on closer examination to be far from all-determining, given that Orientals and black West Indians are more economically successful than some white groups. Other variables commonly overlooked — such as age, location, and fertility — prove to have a major impact on incomes and occupations.

The chapters that follow apply the basic economic principles discussed on pp.4-7 above. It may be well to review them before proceeding.

CHAPTER TWO

The Economics of Discrimination

Like so many words in constant use, discrimination is seldom defined. Familiarity takes the place of precision. Yet, if we are to reason about discrimination in cause-and-effect terms (not merely react to it in moral and emotional terms), then the concept must be made specific. Otherwise, we literally do not know what we are talking about.

The point here is not to derive the one and only possible meaning of the word. Rather, the purpose is to emphasize the importance of sticking to whatever meaning is selected, so that our reasoning is about a *meaning* and not about a *word* which can have many very different meanings. Among the possible meanings of economic discrimination are:

1 The offering of different transactions terms to individuals differing objectively only by group membership, not by any of the criteria commonly used otherwise (such as skill, experience, dependability, etc.). At the extreme, this would include offering *no* transactions terms for some desirable jobs, neighborhoods, or honors.

2 The offering of different transactions terms (including no terms at all) to individuals subjectively perceived as differing in the relevant criteria, but so perceived only because of group membership used as the basis for presumptions about behavior, rather than because of a desire to harm the group, as such. "Unconscious prejudice"

or "institutional racism" are terms that have been used to characterize this pattern.

3   The offering of transactions terms which differ, on the average, among individuals from different group backgrounds. Individuals may be judged honestly and accurately as individuals, but, if the groups themselves differ in the relevant criteria, there will be differences in results.

Much of the controversy over various "equal opportunity" and "affirmative action" programs has been between those who believe that intergroup income, occupational, and other differences are a result of the first (or first two) processes, and those who believe that they are the result of the third. All three situations have undoubtedly existed at various times and places. For analytical purposes, it does not matter with which of these three beliefs one begins. What matters is that they be formulated in such a way as to distinguish them in terms of different empirical results that would be observed when each of them is incorrect. A theory cannot really be proven to be true (something else might have caused the observed phenomenon), but it can be disproven if the observed outcome is incompatible with the theory's implications. In choosing among theories, we tentatively accept the one which survives many opportunities to be disproven.

PURE DISCRIMINATION

Proposition number one above represents the simplest or purest case of discrimination — where people are treated differently because of group membership as such. This is commonly tested by sorting individuals into sets with similar objective characteristics relevant to the transactions, and then seeing if there are still group differences in transactions terms (income, occupation, etc.) within each set. Residual differences after holding other factors constant are then regarded as showing the presence and magnitude of group discrimination. However straightforward and unexceptionable this procedure might be in principle, there are some problems in practice.

First, there is the question of determining which variables are relevant. As noted in chapter 1, age and location have a major impact on income, but have been overlooked in many specifications of possible causes of intergroup differences. Education is a characteristic commonly included on the list of relevant variables, but this raises a question of how finely specified a variable must be, because a year of schooling can represent very different amounts of education, depending upon the number of days in a school year, and the amount and kind of resources used.

For example, it was commonplace at one time for black children in parts of the South to have only two-thirds as many days scheduled per school year as white children. This meant that a black adult with 12 years of schooling had only had as many days in school as a white adult with 8 years of schooling. Holding years of schooling constant did not mean holding education constant. Huge differences in per-pupil expenditures added to the inequality of what was nominally the "same" education. In short, past discrimination against children makes it difficult to measure current discrimination against adults. Both constitute discrimination over some historical span, but some attempt would have to be made to separate them for purposes of determining whether or to what extent there was current employer discrimination.

Even when two groups attended the same schools in the same neighborhood, as Jewish and Italian immigrant children did in the late nineteenth and early twentieth centuries, each brought to the experience an attitude and tradition formed thousands of miles away and hundreds of years before. As a noted historian once said: "We do not live in the past, but the past in us". For centuries, education held a sacred place in the Jewish scheme of values, while in southern Italy *opposition* to formal schooling was so deep-rooted that the first compulsory school attendance laws there provoked riots and even the burning of school houses. In the early immigrant generations, at least, these very different reactions to school meant that equally intelligent youngsters in identical schools received very different amounts of education. The historical and sociological literature is full of accounts of how the one group of immigrant children were the teachers' joy, and the other their despair. Objective data on test scores, graduation rates, etc., confirm vast differences between these American children according to their respective historical and cultural backgrounds in a Europe that most of them never saw.

Group differences need not be hereditary in a biological sense to be real in their impact. While it is necessary to be on guard against stereotypes, one cannot dogmatize that cultural differences do not affect economically relevant variables.

When education is measured by academic performance level reached, rather than by years of schooling completed, racial differences in the return on investment change substantially. As shown in table 2.1, the percentage increase in annual earnings per school year completed is uniformly greater for white males than for black males, but the results are mixed when comparing the percentage increase per year of academic achievement, measured by test scores.

Hispanic males (Mexican Americans and Puerto Ricans)

Table 2.1   Rate of return on education

	Earnings increase per year of schooling (per cent)	Earnings increase per year of academic achievement (per cent)
Black males		
high school or less	3.7	5.1
post-secondary	9.0	8.7
Hispanic males		
high school or less	5.2	7.1
post-secondary	11.9	11.9
White males		
high school or less	4.4	4.6
post-secondary	9.8	9.7

Source: Adapted from Eric Hanushek, "Ethnic Income Variations," *Essays and Data on American Ethnic Groups,* p.157.

average less total education than either blacks or other whites, but receive a higher rate of return than either on what education they have. This is true whether education is measured by years of schooling or by academic achievement. Holding educational achievement constant, the data do not show current employer discrimination in pay among black or Hispanic male, full-time workers born within the United States (excluding Puerto Rico) who constitute the sample for the data in table 2.1. Both black and Hispanic workers have higher than average unemployment rates, so these data do not deal with the other aspect of transactions terms — namely, the extent to which transactions terms are offered at all.

In general, as education is specified progressively more finely, black — white income differences decline, as shown in table 2.2.

Table 2.2   Black individual earnings (as a percentage of white individual earnings)

	per cent
Total	63
College graduates	70
Doctorates in same field	100+

Sources: 1970 Census, Public Use Sample, and Thomas Sowell, *Affirmative Action Reconsidered* (American Enterprise Institute, 1975), pp. 18-20.

The different degrees of fineness with which education can be measured — changing the end results according to the specifications — illustrate a more general problem. Groups that are distributed differently across a scale measuring a relevant variable are probably distributed differently *within* any given interval on the same scale. See figure 2.1. Therefore when we *say* that we are holding the variable constant, we are not in fact doing so. We are only comparing individuals within the same interval, and group averages within the interval will tend to differ if groups are distributed differently across the whole range. As smaller and smaller

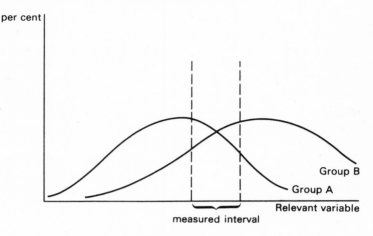

FIGURE 2.1

intervals are taken, we are *approaching* holding the variable constant. If we could know the limit of this process, we would actually know what we are only approximating when we compare individuals from different groups within some interval of education, age-brackets, regional location, etc.

When discrimination is measured as a residual — for example, all income differences remaining after holding age, education, etc., constant — then that residual is in fact the sum of the effects of all unspecified variables plus all inadequately specified variables (the interval problem, the definition of "education", etc.) plus actual discrimination. The residual therefore represents the limit of the effect of discrimination, with perfect specification of all other variables. This discrimination limit is often called simply discrimination, but this is not only incorrect in principle, but especially so where few variables are held constant or specified with precision.

In general, as more variables are held constant or specified more precisely, the income differences between low-income ethnic groups and the national average declines, suggesting that pure discrimination is less than apparent discrimination. The opposite is also possible, however. For example, Chinese American families earn more income than the national average. However, they also have more (and better) education. Moreover, a higher proportion of Chinese families have two or more persons working. When these two factors are held constant, the Chinese income advantage disappears.

In 13 of the 18 comparison cells in table 2.3, Chinese incomes are below those of their counterparts in the general population. Chinese family incomes are above the national average overall because they are distributed differently among the categories. For example, 19 per cent of male-headed Chinese families have three or more income earners, compared to 12 per cent of male-headed families in the general population. One reason for intergroup income

Table 2.3   Family earnings of male-headed families

Education of family head	One income earner per family	Two income earners per family	Three or more income earners per family
Less than high school	$	$	$
Chinese	5,544	8,975	12,327
Total US	5,678	9,144	12,712
High school			
Chinese	7,947	11,681	15,206
Total US	8,616	11,163	15,256
College, 1-3 years			
Chinese	8,771	11,617	18,066
Total US	10,902	12,332	16,981
College, 4 years			
Chinese	11,870	15,428	20,726
Total US	14,521	15,530	19,600
Postgraduate one year			
Chinese	10,296	12,495	30,462
Total US	13,713	14,519	20,646
Postgraduate 2 or more years			
Chinese	17,448	18,792	26,505
Total US	18,810	19,568	22,751

Source: 1970 US Census, Public Use Sample.

differences that is routinely overlooked is that some people work more than others!

Among the possible reasons for the slight Chinese income disadvantage could be discrimination. Other reasons might be their slightly younger age (less experience) or the high proportion of the foreign born among them (less language fluency, contacts, general acculturation).

The main point here is that gross income deficits between a particular group and the "national average" do not prove or measure discrimination — nor do gross income advantages disprove it.

The economics of discrimination involves more than determining its existence or the magnitude of its effects. There are also questions about what kind of economic conditions tend to increase or decrease discrimination. Economics takes as axiomatic the proposition that more of anything is demanded at a low price than at a high price. Discrimination is no exception. A pair of twins might be equally racist, but, if one was an employer of violinists and the other an employer of basketball players, they would face very different costs of excluding blacks. Their subjective *prejudices* might be identical, but economics would predict that the differing costs would produce different amounts of overt *discrimination*. In short, there is a downward sloping demand curve for discrimination.

Looked at another way, there are costs to the discriminator, as well as to the victim, and the magnitude of those costs affects the extent to which subjective prejudices produce overt discrimination. Foregone opportunities to make money — as employer, landlord, seller, lender, etc. — put a price on discrimination. Economic competition means that the less discriminatory transactors acquire a competitive advantage, forcing others either to reduce their discrimination or to risk losing profits, perhaps even being forced out of business. This in turn means that in *less* competitive situations, economic principles would predict that *more* discrimination would exist, because its cost would be less.

At one extreme, a firm operating under a guaranteed cost-plus pricing arrangement — a regulated public utility, for example — would have zero costs of discrimination. All the extra costs entailed by refusing to hire qualified members of particular groups would be passed on to a consuming public with no alternative supplier. Conversely, any savings made by dropping discrimination would be savings to the consumers but not to the public utility, whose profit rate is fixed by the government regulatory commission. Zero discrimination costs in this situation would imply more discrimination in the sense of more severe restrictions on the kinds of jobs available to minorities and more different minorities excluded. For example, in the era before civil rights legislation, telephone companies not only refused to hire blacks in high-level positions, but even as linemen or operators. Moreover, restrictions applied not only to blacks but to Jews, Catholics, and others.

By contrast, a highly competitive industry such as entertainment has traditionally had a disproportionate over-representation of whatever minorities were having difficulties making a career in other fields. Vaudeville, then the record industry, and today television, have been dominated by performers from an ethnic minority background. This is obvious in the case of black performers, but no less true of others, including many whose anglicized stage names conceal their ethnic identity.

Sometimes the objection to a particular ethnic group is not to their mere physical presence or proximity, but to their occupying positions of prosperity, dignity, or authority. They might be acceptable, or even preferred over members of the general population, for menial jobs. Moreover, objections to minorities may originate with the transactor himself or he may be acting because of the racial or ethnic biases of customers, other workers, neighbors, or other individuals or groups. This changes details rather than principles.

PERCEPTUAL DISCRIMINATION

In addition to the kind of discrimination that can occur because of antipathy or animosity toward a racial or ethnic group, there is discrimination that can occur because the group is perceived as less capable or less responsible by employers, landlords, or other potential transactors. Evidence for such a perception may range from zero on upward.

This second kind of discrimination does not invariably accompany the first. Anti-Semitism and anti-Oriental feelings and actions, for example, were often based on a belief that Jews, Chinese, or Japanese were *too* capable — and therefore "unfair" competition for other Americans who could not (or should not be expected to) work so hard and long, or live so frugally to save for the future.

Perceptual discrimination has been exemplified in such historic phrases as "No Irish need apply" or "white only" when the jobs required skills, intelligence, or supervisory responsibilities. It is revealing that the groups especially singled out for this kind of discrimination — blacks, the Irish, and Italians, for example — have typically been from an unskilled rural background, unlike the Jews, for example. As those groups formerly from a peasant or slave background became more urbanized and more familiar with an industrial or commercial economy, the perceptions of their capabilities may have lagged behind the reality of their progress. Moreover, particular individuals whose capabilities advanced faster than their group's capabilities would often tend to be judged by their group average, rather than by their own individual performance. To some extent, this was inevitable, given that knowledge has costs.

Where the perception of the whole group's average performance level is incorrect, several things would tend to happen in a market economy. First, those transactors with more accurate assessments would gain a competitive advantage over those more blinded by prejudice or inertia. This puts a cost on misperceptions, just as there is a cost on discrimination based on pure bigotry. The magnitude of this cost would also vary with the degree of competitiveness of the relevant market. The more competitive the market, the more the costs approach a prohibitive level. In a highly competitive market, any firm paying more for a factor of production, such as labor could have its survival jeopardized.

Similar principles apply in consumer markets of various sorts.

Second, misperceptions provide a special opportunity for economic gains by entrepreneurial members of the group discriminated against. If other transactors misjudge the group's capabilities, or the means of bringing out their potential, those more intimately familiar with the group from the inside can reap extra profit by employing or managing membersof the under-rated group. The Italian American *padrone* in the nineteenth and early twentieth centuries filled such a key role in recruiting and managing Italian immigrant workers, just as Mexican American labor contractors do today. Jewish employers hiring Jewish immigrant workers in New York's nineteenth century garment industry, and Chinese restaurant owners hiring Chinese workers were other examples.

A special case of intragroup reaction to external misperception is individual self-employment. If outsiders have higher knowledge costs of correctly assessing either individual or group capability, there is an extra incentive for misjudged individuals to be employed by those with lower knowledge costs — notably themselves. This self-employment may range from farming to business proprietorship to individual professional practice to such freelancing activities as crime, writing, itinerant entertaining, preaching, or taking in boarders or laundry. All these occupations and activities let an individual's capabilities find their own reward, more or less independently of outside institutional assessments. Ethnic minorities have been notable in all these areas, the particular pattern varying somewhat by group culture.

Because group stereotypes have been common, it is tempting to believe that perceptual discrimination has been widespread. However, articulating a stereotype is cheap, while acting on it can be costly. Moreover, economic analysis cannot proceed on the arbitrary premise that all adverse group perceptions are *mis*perceptions. There is too much evidence of group differences in behavior patterns in too many areas — fertility, attitude toward education, patterns of voting, child-rearing practices, eating habits, etc. — to arbitrarily assume that they are homogeneous in all the relevant variables when they transact in labor, housing, or other markets. It is an empirical question rather than an axiom.

One way of testing whether or to what extent group disadvantages are due to misperceptions is to compare results among culturally different subsets of a group who are *not* perceived differently by employers, landlords, or other transactors in the general population. For example, few transactors in the general American population have been able to distinguish between those Italian Americans whose ancestors orginated in the north of Italy and those whose ancestors originated in the south of Italy. Yet very different cultures and values exist in these two parts of Italy, and there have been large economic differences between immigrants from the two areas, differences not entirely obliterated even among later generations born and raised in America. Northern Italy has had a culture and values more similar to those of the United States, and northern Italians were far more successful in the American economy, especially in business and the professions. Those who were workers were unionized far more often than were southern Italians.

Similar internal cultural differences have existed among other ethnic groups who "all look alike" to outside observers and transactors. Similarly, sharp internal differences exist among Chinese Americans who immigrated to the United States many years ago, primarily from one province in China, and more recent immigrants who have debarked from Hong Kong and originated from all over China. Prosperity and very low crime rates have long been characteristic of the former; desperate poverty and youthful criminal gangs have been characteristic of the latter.

There have been comparable differences among those blacks whose ancestors were (1) free before the Civil War, (2) freed by the Civil War, and who (3) immigrated from the West Indies. As noted in chapter 1, the last named group has an average income comparable to whites. Studies have shown their fertility rates and crime rates to be lower than those of whites.

The point of all these internal group comparisons is that external perceptual discrimination (or other discrimination) cannot explain large economic differences between subsets of a group who "all look alike" to outsiders with whom they transact. Moreover, insofar as the more fortunate segment exceeds the national average, it becmes difficult to explain a below average economic result for the group as a whole in terms of the behavior of external transactors.

Note that this is *not* saying that whenever any members of a disadvantaged group exceed the national average that invalidates all claims of discrimination. The internal group breakdowns here are by *ex ante* social characteristics, not by *ex post* economic results. It was not merely that some Italians, or Chinese, or Negroes turned out to be successful. The point is that whole subsets defined initially by non economic characteristics proved to be economically successful, though largely indistinguishable from their less successful compatriots, as far as outside transactors were concerned.

Misperceptions of individuals may have serious personal consequences, but do not imply *group* discrimination. Where employment, renting, lending, or other transactions decisions are based on assessments that are accurate for the group average but inaccurate for the individual under consideration, the windfall losses of those individuals underestimated by applying the group average are offset by windfall gains by those individuals overestimated by applying the group average. It can be viewed as an internal transfer, rather than a net loss imposed on the group as a whole.

It is tempting to say that each individual should be judged as an individual. But however desirable that might seem in the abstract, no one actually does that in real life, because costs of knowledge make it prohibitive. Even people who imagine themselves to be judging individuals individually are usually doing so only within groups already presorted. Even if every individual encountered on a college campus is judged purely as an individual — without regard to sex or whether he or she is a professor, janitor, student, secretary, or trustee

— that is still not saying that people from the campus are treated the same as people from Skid Row. A shadowy figure lurking in an alley on a dark night is unlikely to be judged as an individual, because the cost of doing so could be one's life. We are more likely to cross the street and walk past, even though it might turn out that the shadowy figure is only a kindly neighbor out walking his dog. In short, even when we consider ourselves to be judging people as individuals, it is usually only after presorting by group or circumstances.

How far should presorting go before judging individuals? There is no categorical answer. It is an incremental decision, based on the changing incremental costs and incremental benefits of doing so. Whether race or ethnicity is a valid presorting category is a many-sided question. From the standpoint of Pareto optimality for the economy, this presorting category cannot be categorically eliminated for the benefit of ethnic minority individuals without increasing knowledge costs, thereby reducing efficiency and therefore imposing losses on other people, who are no less real or important because they may not be part of some readily recognizable group. On the other hand, the very existence of a society implies some sense of justice, and choosing cost-bearers on the basis of race or ethnicity goes counter to general conceptions of justice, thereby imposing costs on the population at large. Even from a more narrowly economic perspective, if individuals from some racial or ethnic backgrounds find doors closed without regard to their individual capabilities and behavior, that reduces their incentves to acquire socially valued capabilities and behavior, imposing external costs on society at large from the decisions of particular employers, landlords, and other transactors.

The point here is not to answer the question of individual versus group judgments, but to suggest its complexities in general, and in particular to point out that the ideal of judging each individual as an individual has costs so high as to make the precept rarely applied in practice, at least not in the categorical sense in which it is asserted. What happens when laws attempt to eliminate group sorting is a cause-and-effect question for later chapters.

SUMMARY

Intergroup economic differences loosely ascribed to "discrimination" result from at least three distinct social phenomena: (1) *antagonism* toward particular groups, expressed economically in an unwillingness to transact with them on terms available to other individuals with the same relevant characteristics, (2) a general *misperception* of the extent to which particular groups possess the economically relevant characteristics, and (3) intergroup *differences* in the economically relevant characteristics, leading to income and occupation results corresponding to such differences.

These distinctions must be kept in mind in the analysis of job markets, consumer markets, and government regulation.

CHAPTER THREE

Job Markets

Job markets range from the theoretically perfect markets found only in textbooks to markets in which pay and employment are largely determined by forces from outside the economic sphere, through political decisions of government. Rather than attempt to deal separately with all the various gradations of markets, we can distinguish two main types: the competitive market and the non-competitive market. We can then analyze the effects of third-party intervention in each kind of market, by government, unions, or employer associations.

COMPETITIVE MARKETS

The defining characteristics of a competitive market are:

1 Sufficiently *large numbers* of independent transactors to (a) prevent effective collusion among either sellers or buyers, and (b) make each individual transactor's share of total transactions too small to affect the prices in the market.

2 Sufficient *knowledge* of offers and bids to prevent different transactions terms from persisting indefinitely in the same market.

3 Sufficient *mobility* of both sets of transactors to prevent different transactions terms from persisting indefinitely in the same market.

In a theoretically perfect market, these requirements are carried to an extreme impossible to reach in the real world: (1) *infinite* numbers of transactors, (2) *perfect* knowledge by all transactors and potential transactors, at zero cost, and (3) *unlimited* mobility at zero cost. In addition, the transactors are all homogeneous with respect to economic characteristics and with respect to each other's perceptions and preferences. These extreme postulates serve to simplify the analysis by eliminating the complications entailed by (1) the varying costs of collusion among various numbers and kinds of transactors, (2) widely varying amounts of knowledge among transactors on both sides, (3) varying mobility costs among numerous transactors, and (4) varying degrees of objective heterogeneity and its subjective perceptions by other transactors.

The elimination of these complicating possibilities by using extreme postulates allows the basic analysis to be presented in its skeletal simplicity. Once this underlying skeleton is understood as determining the basic form, then the flesh-and-blood complications of reality can be added — enriching, but not fundamentally changing, that form.

In economic analysis, the real-world complications often change the end result only trivially, but this cannot be assumed at the outset. In some instances involving ethnic minorities, the differences due to heterogeneity of characteristics, perceptions, or preferences (including racism) can be substantial or even overwhelming.

The requirement of "large numbers" for competitive market results is to exclude deliberately controlled economic results, which are possible when a substantial share of transactions can be offered or withheld at the discretion of one individual or coalition. But just how large these "large numbers" would have to be to achieve competitive results may vary with respect to the kind of transactions involved. The cost of a collusive coalition varies with what they are colluding about. The weakness of economic coalitions — whether producer cartels or employer associations — is that what is optimal for the individual member differs from what is optimal for the coalition as a whole. In a cartel, for example, individual profit maximization is achieved when charging a lower price than agreed upon, and selling more than one's assigned quota, while other members of the cartel honor the agreement. Cartels and other coalitions must therefore police their agreements.

Discriminatory Collusion

The analytic significance of collusion costs is that the same firms that may be competitive for some purposes (with high collusion costs) may be non-competitive for other purposes (with low collusion costs). The policing of an agreement not to hire blacks is easier than policing an agreement not to hire Scandinavians, or an agreement not to make deliveries on Sunday, or not to make rebates or other price concessions that are difficult to monitor. The coalition can take whatever retaliatory measures are available when a realtor violates an agreement not to rent or sell to blacks in certain neighborhoods — such agreement being both legal and common before "restrictive covenants" were declared illegal in 1948. On economic grounds, the history of especially severe discrimination against blacks and Orientals may reflect in part the low cost of policing an agreement where skin color differences are involved.

Policing costs are not the sole economic consideration in the success or failure of collusion attempts, however. The major cost is the cost of foregone opportunities for profitable transactions. If these potential profits are sufficiently large, it may be worth braving retaliation to obtain them, so that an economic coalition to discriminate may fail even when there are low costs of policing transactions with people of a different skin color.

Perhaps the classic attempts of this sort were post-Civil War coalitions of white employers to keep down the pay of newly freed blacks. If ever an employer cartel had all apparent advantages, this one did. Not only could the victims be readily detected by skin color, blacks at that time were almost all unable to read or write or — more important economically — count. The law would not even protect their physical safety, much less their rights. Many became sharecroppers, who put their X on contracts they could not read, and traded at company stores at prices they did not know. For some unscrupulous employers, it was a golden opportunity to cheat on a massive scale — for a while. But even people unable to detect specific numerical cheating, or other ways in which they were taken advantage of, nevertheless knew when friends or relatives working for other employers (or sharecropping with other landowners) were living better than they were. They were unable to receive retrospective justice, but they were able to change their prospective behavior.

Higher paying employers and landowners found more people applying to work for them, and were able to take their pick of the best workers available. Lower paying employers found their vacancies harder to fill, and cheating landowners had difficulties finding enough sharecroppers to farm their land. Their choices were to raise pay or lose profits. They raised pay. The net result was that in the period between the Civil War and the end of the nineteenth century, black incomes rose at a higher rate than white incomes. Sharecropper contract terms also changed to the benefit of blacks, even though many could not read them. Southern newspapers and magazines were full of recriminations among white employers because they failed to stick together in resisting the pressure of higher pay for blacks. Even though blacks were unorganized, and could have voiced no strong explicit demands if they had been, given the repressive environment of the times, nevertheless their "voting with their feet" achieved the same net result. Although economists postulate perfect knowledge in an ideal labor market, a very small amount of knowledge of alternatives can produce very similar end results in equalizing wages in comparable occupations and relating pay to marginal product.

The crucial element in destroying economic coalitions are the opportunities for profit by individual members who violate the solidarity of the coalition. In situations where there are few opportunities for profit, the collusion may be successful even when there are only minor sanctions available, perhaps no more than social pressures. Exclusions against black violinists could be maintained much more cheaply than discrimination against black sharecroppers in the past or black basketball players today. In short, the supply of qualified transactors determines the cost of maintaining exclusions and discrimination. What then determines the supply of qualified applicants, especially for jobs from which they are known to be excluded?

Where a particular job requires a long or costly preparation to develop skills applicable only in that occupation, then the very existence of the barrier discourages any such investment from being undertaken in the first place. Therefore it is unlikely that there will ever be such a build-up of qualified applicants from the excluded group as to make it profitable for individual employers to breech the exclusion. In short, a relatively weakly policed or weakly sanctioned exclusion may hold under these conditions, whereas a more readily policed and heavily sanctioned barrier may give way when there are more numerous qualified applicants, representing opportunities for more substantial profits.

In some cases, the skills needed in an ethnically or racially restricted occupation are also used in other occupations, so that investments are made in the relevant skills despite the exclusions. The resulting backlog of qualified applicants then provides an incentive for individual employers to violate the exclusion agreement — and once the exclusion is breeched, competitive pressures tend to expand the breech and even eliminate the exclusion entirely within a relatively few years. For example, Jews were excluded from the faculties of many top-rated universities until World War II. Yet many Jews acquired academically usable skills in their preparation for other occupations in science, medicine, or the arts and letters generally. When the post-World War II shortage of college teachers forced some leading institutions to hire Jews for the first time, competing holdouts had little choice but to follow suit, and within a relatively few years Jews became *over-*represented (as a per cent of the population) in leading university faculties — and remain so.

Something similar happened in professional sports which once excluded black athletes. Recreational and college varsity athletics continued to attract and develop black athletes, despite the professional exclusion. Moreover, black professional leagues were organized, notably in baseball, providing another avenue for the development of professional skills and another occupation in which to employ them. When the Brooklyn Dodgers hired the first black athlete (Jackie Robinson) in 1947, and added two more black stars in 1949, they acquired a competitive advantage which other teams could not allow to continue indefinitely. Within a few years the color line collapsed in other teams, and so many black athletic stars were hired that for seven consecutive years no white man won the National League's Most Valuable Player award. Similar patterns emerged in other professional sports.

The rigid exclusion, holding perfectly for years and then suddenly collapsing completely after once being breeched, has not been limited to Jews in the academic world or blacks in sports. The expansion of a ghetto neighborhood boundary has often followed a similar pattern. A certain street may form an impenetrable barrier for years, but once the excluded group rents or buys on the other side of that line, the whole neighborhood may relatively quickly change its ethnic or racial composition. The build-up of qualified excluded applicants in this case is a build-up of *financially* qualified people as a continued influx of people into the constricted ghetto creates a pent-up demand for more housing.

External Controls
Competitive markets as they exist in the real world differ from theoretically perfect textbook models in many ways that are sometimes trivial and sometimes substantial in their effects. The infinitely large numbers of transactors with infinitely small individual shares of market transactions, which make collusion costs prohibitive in the theoretical model, turn out in the real world to mean varying collusion costs which can make the same set of firms price-competitive in the product market and racially collusive in the labor market. Similarly, the perfectly homogeneous labor force of the theoretical model, which eliminates the complications of sorting costs and ethnic (and other) preferences, turns out in the real world to mean that the ethnic preferences of customers and co-workers are reflected in employers' hiring and promotion decisions, along with the employer's own preferences and perceptions. The competitiveness of the

market puts a price on discrimination, thereby reducing but not necessarily eliminating it.

In addition to decisions deliberately based on or influenced by ethnicity, there are also institutional modifications of competitive markets whose net effects affect the pay and employment of racial or ethnic minorities, even though the actual purposes of these institutional modifications may have had nothing to do with race or ethnicity. For example, a government imposed or union imposed wage rate above the market equilibrium level (see figure 3.1) creates a surplus of job applicants $(L_2 - L_1)$ making discrimination virtually costless. The employer is free to indulge whatever prejudices he may have against however many groups there may be, as long as all the excluded groups put together are no larger proportion of the job applicants than the jobs (L_1) are of the applicants (L_2). The purpose of the imposed wage increase may have been to benefit the workers, but the effect is not limited to the intentions.

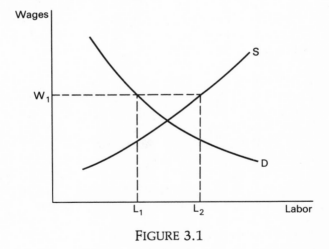

FIGURE 3.1

Conversely, when wage rates are held artificially low by third party intervention (see figure 3.2), this creates a labor shortage $(L_4 - L_3)$, thereby *raising* the cost of discrimination. Comprehensive wartime wage controls, as during World War II, may have this effect. Many occupations were in fact opened up to previously excluded minorities during World War II's labor shortages. This apparently had some long-run effect on perceptual discrimination, as many employers discovered higher capabilities than they had thought among newly hired minorities.

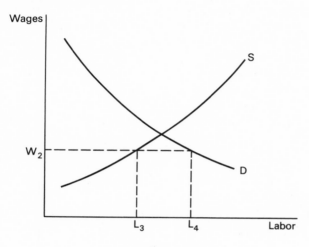

FIGURE 3.2

Occupational licensing can also affect ethnic minorities in a special way. Where licensing is merely a routine process for determining if applicants are qualified for particular occupations, its economic effects may be negligible. However, *restrictive* licensing — where the number of licenses is limited, regardless of how many qualified applicants exist — creates a different situation (see figure 3.3). The number of restricted licenses (L_5) is less than the number of jobs that would exist in equilibrium (L_6), in order to force up the pay to higher levels (W_3) than would exist in equilibrium. The higher wage in turn attracts even more applicants (L_7) than would exist in unrestricted market equilibrium. Again, this permits virtually costless discrimination, as long as those applicants discriminated against do not exceed the size of the surplus.

The extent to which this discriminatory potential will be exercised depends upon whether the restricted license is saleable by the owner. Licenses to drive a taxi may be sold but licenses to practice surgery cannot. Where there is a non-saleable license, then the licensing agency can discriminate against various groups at negligible cost, according to its own antipathies or those of the incumbent licensees. Discrimination against Jewish or Negro doctors was common at one time in admissions to medical school or hospital practice.

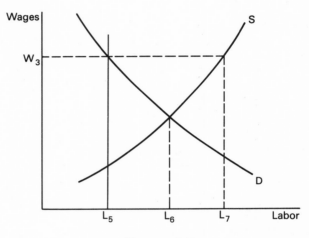

FIGURE 3.3

Where the restricted license is saleable, the situation is different (see figure 3.4). The license itself acquires a market value — sometimes running into many thousands of dollars — and may be owned by the employer. In the case of a restricted license to operate a taxicab, the amount paid to the driver (W_5) by the passenger is less than the amount that the driver is allowed to keep (W_4) by the license owner. If the driver owns his own license (rare in a city like New York, where taxi licenses cost about $60,000) when he is earning $W_5 - W_4$ as a property owner and only W_4 as a cab driver.

Note that under these circumstances the net wages (W_4) of the licensed workers are *less* than they would be under unrestricted competition, because fewer workers are demanded to fill the restricted number of jobs. Moreover, there are no surplus applicants at the artificially low wage rate. For the license owners to discriminate against either potential workers or potential purchasers of licenses would be to reduce their own profits from the use or sale of the license. Excluding various categories of workers would mean shifting the supply curve of eligible workers to the left, raising the wages that would have to be paid out of the same gross earnings, thereby reducing the difference between W_5 and W_4. That difference represents current income from the license, and its capitalized value is the sale price of the license. The reduction of that income from the license would be the cost of discrimination to the discriminator.

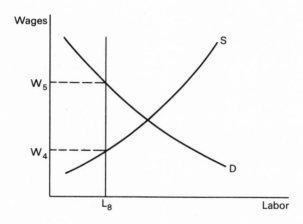

FIGURE 3.4

Internal Controls
The abstract, theoretically perfect, labor market of textbook models would lack many of the phenomena of real world competition. For example, with zero mobility costs and zero knowledge costs (omniscience), each worker would change jobs instantly in response to the tiniest wage rate differential, moving about from job to job several times in the course of a single day, until equilibrium was reached. Employers in turn would have to be constantly looking for people to fill vacancies. The rushing about in labor markets would

resemble the frantic motions of the old Keystone Kops movies.

Clearly this does not happen in the real world because both employers and employees recognize that there are transactions costs and search costs. Employers, in particular, are likely to want to make the relationship lasting by holding out prospective benefits for longtime employees. One way is to hire from the bottom, for lower skill jobs, and promote from within the firm to fill higher level positions. By providing prospects for advancement, the firm expects to reduce labor turnover.

How does this affect ethnic minorities? Those minorities with less skill or experience, or perceived as having less, become less employable than when each job (high or low) was filled separately. Once the low level jobs become such rungs on a job ladder, the qualifications for such an entry level position reflect not only the requirements of that job itself, but of jobs further up the ladder. People deemed unpromotable become unemployable, even though perfectly qualified to do the kind of work in which there is a vacancy.

Where people are hired according to their qualifications for the actual vacancy, with no requirements based on their potential for a prearranged sequence of promotions, clearly more people will be employable. Nineteenth-century immigrants from a peasant background, lacking industrial skills or experience (and sometimes unable to speak English), were nevertheless employable in unskilled manual jobs. All that mattered was whether they could fill the existing vacancy — not whether they were considered promising material for higher level jobs. Today, comparable workers from rural Southern backwoods do not find steady employment as readily available. Partly this is because "dead-end jobs" are less available. The pejorative term, "dead-end jobs", falsely insinuates that the individual worker cannot advance, simply because there is no prearranged job promotion pattern, with its attendant difficulties of finding initial employment. Much upward mobility takes the form of changing jobs or even employers, rather than being promoted in a prearranged pattern. So-called "dead-end jobs" are especially important for younger workers not yet accustomed to the requirements of working in general — punctuality, dependability, cooperation with co-workers and supervisors, etc. Simple as these things may seem, they often take considerable time to develop and become habitual. "Dead-end jobs" are places where an individual can both develop such work habits and acquire a personal track record for having them — making him more valuable to other employers and for higher level jobs. That there is no prearranged sequence or timetable for promotion means that each individual's progress is a function of his own development. The more disadvantaged, unskilled, or misperceived an ethnic group is, the more valuable such jobs are, for their young people especially.

Another practice that made nineteenth-century job markets more like those of a competitive model — and nineteenth-century immigrants more employable than twentieth-century minorities — was payment by output rather than by time at work. In the theoretically perfect labor market, with homogeneous labor and zero cost of knowing its capabilities, paying piece rates would be no different from paying hourly wages. In a world of heterogeneous labor and substantial costs of finding out its efficiency through trial and error, paying according to the quantity of each worker's output reduces the risks when hiring workers who are untried (and perhaps suspected of being substandard). In short, the competitive model's end results of paying equal wages for equal productivity is approximated more closely with piece rates than with hourly wages.

Those workers whose skills and capabilities are most questionable, or most difficult for an employer to assess because of language or other cultural differences, are particularly affected by the difference between hourly pay and piece-rate pay. They are most likely not to be employed when they offer to sell their time rather than offer to sell their output. Even if they are in fact less productive, that is less of a hiring handicap where their pay will automatically reflect that difference than when it will not. Piece-rate payment was much more common in the nienteenth-century labor markets than in the twentieth-century labor markets, and ninenteenth-century minorities were more likely to be considered "overworked" rather than chronically unemployed.

Another nineteenth-century labor market pattern that has largely disappeared, through legislation and unionization, was the practice of having workers work at home. By not having to provide as large a workplace for a given number of employees, the employer saved on capital costs — a saving sometimes made even more substantial when the worker supplied his own tools, which might range from hammers to sewing machines. This arrangement had the further advantage of not requiring people of different racial or ethnic backgrounds to have to get along at the workplace. In short, it reduced the cost of intergroup prejudices — the employers' or fellow workers' — and made minorities more employable. Home work was of course paid by piece rates, further relieving the employer of any concern over group or individual capabilities, and therefore making more disadvantaged ethnic groups employable. The risks of damage to tools by unskilled employees was also reduced by having the worker supply his own, just as the risk of damage to efficiency by intergroup friction was reduced by having the workers separated in their own respective homes.

The home-work system was used not only for light industrial work — New York's garment industry being perhaps the classic exampe — but also for such things as low-income housewives taking in laundry or sewing. These latter were common patterns among the Irish in the nineteenth-century, and among blacks on into the twentieth-century.

NON-COMPETITIVE MARKETS

In addition to profit-maximizing competitive employers, ethnic minorities (and others) can be hired by employers whose profits are externally constrained (a regulated public utility), or who are legally non-profit (colleges, hospitals, foundations), or by the government.

The simplest case is the firm legally prohibited from earning any profit. Because one of the main costs of discrimination is foregone profits from transacting with the otherwise undesired group, to remove profit as a consideration is to lower the cost of discrimination. There may be some residual cost of discrimination, if either the law or public opinion requires the pretense of considering each applicant, or perhaps at least "token" hiring. However, both of these latter considerations are relatively recent in history, and before their appearance there was a virtually zero cost of discrimination to non-profit organizations. Economic theory would predict that employment discrimination would be at its peak in non-profit organizations. That is also what the historical record suggests.

Discrimination levels in colleges, universities, hospitals, and the government itself were, in past eras, greater than in competitive industries at the same time. As of 1936, for example, only three black Ph.D.s were employed by all the white universities in the United States, whereas 300 black chemists alone were employed in private industry. Prior to World War II, it was common for hospitals to allow neither black nor Jewish doctors on their staffs. Philanthropic foundations generally did not hire blacks, even when the foundations' avowed purpose was the advancement of blacks. In the government, blacks were only 1 per cent of non-Postal Civil Service workers in 1930 and there were no blacks at all in the navy.

Profit-constrained public utilities were very similar. Although they were legally permitted to earn profits, the amounts earned were held below the market level by regulatory commissions. Therefore any increased costs they might incur by discriminatory hiring practices simply forced prices up toward what they would have been under profit maximization. In the classic "natural monopoly" case of a regulated public utility (see figure 3.5), the unconstrained equilibrium price would be P_2, but the regulatory agency sets some lower price, P_1. The regulated firm therefore has an incentive to let its costs rise toward P_2 as long as the regulatory agency will allow prices to rise accordingly, passing on to the customers (who have no alternative supplier) the cost of various amenities and indulgences for the management of the utility.

Here, too, empirical evidence supports what economic

theory implies. Perhaps the classic examples were the railroad occupations, where blacks in the South were generally *over*represented in the nineteenth-century *before* federal regulation and widespread unionization, and then *totally excluded* from most railroad occupations afterwards. When railroads were unconstrained profit-maximizers, the opportunity cost of discrimination was high. Later, as a regulated utility, high union pay scales created a chronic surplus of applicants, and the costs of discrimination were virtually zero.

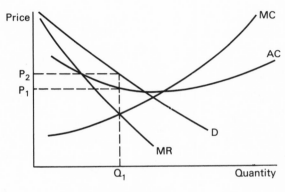

FIGURE 3.5

While non-profit organizations, regulated utilities, and the government have been relatively free of economic constraints in their policies toward ethnic minorities, they have been especially subject to political incentives or constraints. Public opinion is very important to all these kinds of institutions, though in different ways. What this means is that the cost of being *either* discriminatory or preferential toward minorities is especially low for such institutions. On economic grounds, one would expect their policies to go further in either direction than the policies of profit-maximizing firms in competitive industries. Which direction would depend on the climate of public opinion in the particular era. Again, history confirms these implications of economic analysis.

In the era of increasing racial and ethnic animosities, dating from around the beginning of the twentieth-century through the 1920s, employment patterns followed such other contemporary developments as widespread race riots, drastic restrictions on immigration, and the re-emergence of the Ku Klux Klan, spreading now into northern cities and widening its victims to include Jews and Catholics as well as blacks. During this era, the federal government began introducing racial segregation among its employees where it had never existed before, and began reducing its employment of blacks in general, and especially in high level positions. One indication of this trend is that there were only half as many black postmasters by the 1930s as there had been in 1910. The requirement that photographs accompany civil service applications was first introduced in this era, along with a change in policy from hiring the top scoring applicant to choosing among the top three. The navy stopped accepting blacks altogether, even though historically there had been large numbers of blacks in the navy during the Civil War and substantial numbers even in the War of 1812. The army followed similar policies to almost the same extremes.

Although there was a clear trend toward increasing discrimination in the federal government in the 1910-1930 era, paralleling national political sentiment, there was no comparable retrogression in private competitive industries during the same era. And in many northern cities, where the number of black voters was increasing by leaps and bounds during the same era, politics pointed in the opposite direction. The number of black municipal employees in New York City, for example, increased more than ninefold from 1917 to 1929. Historically, various ethnic minorities have at one time or other been overrepresented among municipal employees after acquiring political strength. The Irish in Boston and New York were classic examples, after building political machines in both cities in the nineteenth-century.

Decades later, after national political sentiment turned against discrimination and in favor of ethnic minorities, the swing of the pendulum was greater in non-profit organizations, public utilities, and the government. Blacks now became *over*represented in both the military and the civilian branches of the federal government. Blacks in the academic world received more job offers and higher pay than whites with comparably ranked Ph.Ds and the same number of publications. The landmark *Bakke* decision grew out of preferential admissions of blacks to a university medical school, and academic institutions across the country filed *amicus curiae* briefs because such policies had become widespread. Again, this illustrates how the same institutions that are most discriminatory in one era tend to be the most preferential under changed political conditions. Indeed, discrimination and preferential treatment are simply two ways of looking at the same phenomenon: being preferential to A, B, and C is the same as being discriminatory toward X, Y, and Z.

The *state* regulated telephone industry is an even better barometer of political pressures because of the widely differing policies of telephone companies in different states during the 1960s, even though most belonged to the same national corporation, A.T. & T. Minority hiring was politically popular in the north before it was in the south. In the north, *one-third* of new telephone company employees hired between 1966 and 1968 were black, but in the South there was no significant change in racial proportions, even though employment was growing faster in the South, providing more opportunities for change there. This regional pattern also existed in gas and electric public utilities.

In short, those employers who were not profit-maximizers have tended to swing further in the direction of whatever prevailing opinion happened to be, as regards ethnic minorities, whether that opinion was discriminatory or preferential. This is what economic analysis would predict, given that the costs of either discrimination or preference are lowest for such employers.

INTENTIONAL VERSUS SYSTEMIC REASONING

Much discussion of employment discrimination has been sprinkled with such terms as "racism", "bigotry", "exploitation", and other pejorative words. Whatever the appropriateness of such terms in a moral context, they add little to a cause-and-effect analysis, and can in fact be very misleading as to the causal mechanisms at work. If those causal mechanisms are misunderstood, policies designed to correct the situation can make things worse.

The intentions of individuals set events in motion, but what course events will take depends upon a complex of circumstances beyond the control of anyone. Economists as different as Adam Smith and Karl Marx have recognized this. Smith referred to the individual contributing to economic results "which were no part of his intention".[1] The Marxian view was reflected in Engels' statement, "what each individual wills is obstructed by everyone else, and what emerges is something that no one wills".[2] Theory is meant to predict "what emerges", not what people intended. It is therefore not a study of their psychological propensities but of surrounding constraints, relationships, and incentives.

CHAPTER FOUR

Consumer Markets

In various ways, ethnic minorities have often faced different consumer market conditions — different transactions terms — from those facing the population at large. Typically, this has meant higher prices, lower quality, or — particularly in the case of housing — no transactions at all in some places. In the brutal language of an earlier era, some apartment houses in turn-of-the-century New York carried the sign: "No dogs, No Jews". Similar policies have been expressed, in varying language, as regards blacks, the Irish, and others, depending upon the time and place.

Consumer markets for ordinary day-to-day purchases of food, clothing, appliances, and amenities have likewise presented different transactions terms (including no transactions at all) to different groups. Among the cause-and-effect questions raised by such phenomena are:

1 To what extent have different transactions terms represented cost differentials in serving particular groups, and to what extent discrimination?

2 How can discriminatory differentials persist in the face of competition?

3 Is it Pareto optimal or otherwise socially beneficial to modify these transactions by government policy?

Several kinds of markets will be considered. The first will be those markets in which many groups were first isolated and treated as minorities — the markets associated with their immigration to America: markets for lodging and food in their ports of embarkation in Europe, markets for passage to America, and markets for lodging and food in their ports of debarkation. Next will be considered ethnic neighborhood markets for ordinary purchases of groceries and other goods and services, and ethnic businesses serving the outside world. Finally, the special market for housing will be considered.

TRAVEL TO AMERICA

Price
For millions of individuals from many different ethnic groups, one of the largest — and certainly most fateful — purchases of their lives was ocean passage to America. In the era of wind-driven ships, the cost of this passage varied enormously even from European countries comparable distances away. Was this price-discrimination or a reflection of cost differentials? The numerous ships and shipping companies involved seem to preclude the monopolistic market conditions required for persistent price discrimination. Cost differentials are much more apparent.

From many parts of Europe, passenger fares would have to cover the average cost of an ocean voyage, whereas from other parts of the continent, passenger fares need only cover the marginal cost. There was a large amount of commercial trade between the United States and various countries in northern and western Europe. The goods shipped from the United States were chiefly agricultural and timber products, while those goods sent back to the US were largely manufactured items. While such trade would tend to balance in value terms, the sheer physical size of the shipments were quite different in the two directions. American goods took up far more cargo space than European goods. This meant that cargo vessels returning from northern and western Europe had empty cargo space, and found it profitable to carry immigrants at any fare that covered the marginal costs incurred by making special provision for human cargo on board. The fares were thus much lower on cargo vessels (where fares covered marginal costs) than on passenger vessels (where fares had to cover average costs). Geographically, that meant that fares were much lower in northern and western Europe than in southern and eastern Europe, during the era of wind-driven ships. History confirms what economic theory would predict, that more immigration to America occurred where it was cheaper during this era — namely, from northern and western Europe (see figure 4.1).

American ethnic groups from northern and western Europe — Anglo-Saxons, Germans, the Irish, etc. — began their adjustment to American life generations before peoples of Italian, Polish, or eastern European Jewish ancestry. As of the early twentieth-century, the former groups — the "old" immigrants, as they were called — were as a group economically, educationally, and socially well in advance of the "newer" immigrant groups. Such intergroup disparities were commonly attributed, at the time, to genetic differences — and, later, to discriminatory treatment. The further passage of time tended to reduce these disparities, suggesting that it was a transitional phenomenon, based on the length of group residence in the United States, and that in turn based on the economic differences in costs of transportation from different parts of Europe. That one of the eastern European groups — the Jews — now tops the list of American ethnic groups in incomes and occupations suggests that neither genetics nor discrimination had the effects attributed, at a time when Jews were among those scoring lower on mental tests and living in poverty in crowded slums.

With the development of steamships, the average cost of crossing the ocean on passenger vessels was brought down within the reach of masses of people previously priced out of the market. The data suggest that the predominance of northern and western Europeans among earlier immigrants did not reflect greater demand there for passage to America, but only lower prices on a given demand curve. After steamships lowered prices everywhere, the quantity of trips purchased in southern and eastern Europe was greater than in northern and western Europe.

In the middle of the nineteenth century, more than 95 per cent of the immigrants arriving in New York came in wind-

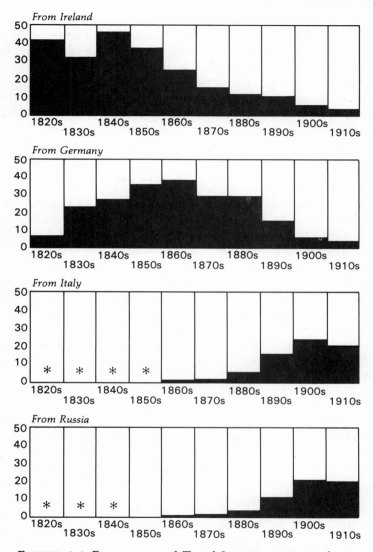

FIGURE 4.1 *Percentage of Total Immigration to the United States*

*Negligible: less than 0.5 percent.
Source: Essays and Data on American Ethnic Groups, p.108.

driven ships, but, in the last quarter of the century, almost all came in steamships. This technological change, which reduced price, increased quantity greatly. The total number of immigrants before the Civil War was 5 million. In the next 30 years, 10 million immigrated. The change in composition was even more dramatic. Whereas 87 per cent of the immigrants were from northern and western Europe in 1882, by 1901 southern and eastern Europeans constituted 81 per cent of the immigrants.

Product Quality

The ocean passage of the nineteenth-century immigrant was very much unlike an ocean voyage today. Most of the people who came to America were unable to afford good quality accommodations, even by the standards of their time. In the steamship era, they came in steerage — crowded, ill-ventilated, and unsanitary. In the era of the wind-driven ships, it was worse, and the voyage lasted longer, taking more of a toll of health and often life itself. In that era, about 10 per cent of the immigrants died *en route*.[1]

Some idea of product quality may be gathered from a contemporary account of what greeted a typical immigrant of the 1840s:

> The emigrant is shown a berth, a shelf of coarse pinewood, situated in a noisome dungeon, airless and lightless, in which several hundred persons of both sexes and all ages are stowed away on shelves two feet one inch above the other, three feet wide and six feet long, still reeking from the ineradicable stench left by the emigrants of the last voyage.[2]

Although there was clearly vast room for improvement, the question is not whether a given product meets some quality standard as defined by third parties, without regard to cost. The question is whether, within the set of possibilities actually available under given constraints of technology and wealth, there are options that would be considered better by those who pay the costs and reap the benefits. The immigrants knew that there were better accommodations available — sometimes on the very same ship — at higher prices. Yet even the very low prices of ocean passage in the hold of wind-driven cargo ships — about ten to twenty shillings[3] — priced the voyage beyond the means of the poorest classes and left many others destitute upon arrival in America.

The economic issue is much more general than ocean voyages, immigrants, or ethnicity, though in this case it was raised in a particularly poignant situation. Contemporary observers, especially those from higher income classes, were profoundly offended and disturbed by the voyage conditions of the masses of poor immigrants, and demanded government intervention. But when the government prohibited certain "bad" conditions, that prohibition in no way enlarged the set of options already available to immigrants and shippers. On the contrary, it eliminated some options without creating any new ones. In general, economic theory would lead one to expect better consumer satisfaction — by the consumer's own preference pattern — from a choice made from a larger set of options, when that larger set contains all the options included in an alternative smaller set.

An empirical test of this principle can be constructed, based upon observable consumer behavior revealing consumer preferences. In the case of British government regulation of voyage conditions among poor Irish immigrants in the 1840s, the law "improving" voyage conditions was passed in 1847 and scheduled to take effect in the spring of 1848. If the better conditions and higher fares were a trade-off that left immigrants indifferent, their observed behavior would show no change in the volume or timing of their voyages. If they preferred the better conditions, at a higher fare entailed by the costs of creating improvements, then the volume of immigration immediately before the law went into effect would be expected to decline and to increase immediately afterward, as some immigrants rescheduled their voyages to acquire their preferred option. (With zero transactions costs and zero time preference, they would all do so, but such extreme assumptions are unnecessary for the argument.) If the immigrants preferred the lower fares to the improvement, then the volume of immigration immediately before the law went into effect would be expected to increase, and then to decline immediately afterward, as immigrants rescheduled their voyages to leave earlier and avoid the "benefits" the government had created for them. This last pattern was what was in fact observed.[4]

"Improving" voyage conditions for Irish emigrants involved particularly painful trade-offs, for there was a massive famine in Ireland at the time, and being able to escape that was clearly for many far more important than any incremental improvements in voyage conditions decreed by a well-fed British parliament, or desired by equally well-fed social reformers.

What ultimately improved voyage conditions while maintaining — and increasing — the volume of immigration, was technological advancement that made lower costs possible, and the forces of competition which made them necessary. The total costs of immigration included not only the voyage itself, but the travel to a commercial port, and the unpredictable length of time spent in temporary lodgings there, waiting to get on sailing ships whose arrivals and departures were both too much dependent upon weather conditions to permit a fixed schedule. The development of steamships introduced predictability of schedules, reducing the waiting time both in port and on the ocean, thereby reducing the costs of food, lodgings, and lost working time. With passenger steamships available in many ports, it was also no longer necessary to travel long distances to a few ports serving the commercial cargo ships that provided marginal cost fares to America. In short, it was the creation of more options by the economy that improved the product and made it accessible to more people — not the reduction of their options by government.

Financing the Voyage
Cheap as a seventeenth-century, eighteenth- or nineteenth-century ocean voyage might seem by modern standards, it was beyond the resources of most of the people of the time. Even after the development of large-scale commercial trade put marginal cost fares within the reach of many in northern

and western Europe, it remained true that the poorest classes of the Irish in the 1840s famine era could not raise enough money to leave, even when remaining meant a substantial risk of death by starvation.

Yet, in the broad sweep of history, the mass emigration to America was, as one historian put it, "the greatest folk-migration in human history".[5] Over the centuries, more than 45 million people came to the United States, from every part of the world. Somehow, ways were found by all those millions to finance the voyage. For some it required years of saving or the liquidation of all personal assets. For many others, even that was not enough. In one way or another, they had to draw upon the assets of others.

Clearly, the conventional lending institutions, such as local banks, would have little incentive to invest in innumerable small loans to people who would be 3,000 miles away when repayment became due. The transactions costs alone would be enormous, because so many transactions would be needed to lend a total volume of money that might be relatively moderate in terms of commercial business loans or investments. Risk costs would also be high, not only because of the great distance between borrower and lender, but also because the borrowers would have been scattered across a vast area in the new world, much of it wilderness in the early centuries. In short, solution of the repayment problem was central to the prospects of immigrants to acquire the assets of others to finance their voyage.

One solution was to acquire assets from those who would either not have to be repaid or who would have little difficulty in locating the person to whom assets had been lent. Family members already in America met these criteria. Among poorer immigrants such as the Irish, family members already in America financed a substantial part of the subsequent immigration. In 1830-1845, from about a third to perhaps half of the Irish immigrants had their passages paid by money from America.[6] This proportion rose to about three-quarters after the famine struck Ireland and Irish-Americans tried desperately to rescue their relatives from a situation in which people were literally dying in the streets. Over a twenty-year period beginning in the 1840s more than

$120 million dollars was transferred by individuals in America to individuals in Ireland.[7]

Long before there were enough relatives in America to finance many ocean voyages, some way to acquire others' assets had to be found by many who came to colonial America and the early United States. The same problems of transactions costs and risks had to be resolved. What evolved in the market was the system known as indentureship. The prospective immigrant contracted in Europe to perform a given number of years of labor in America (usually about 4 or 5 years), in exchange for ocean passage. Either the lender was located in America or the contract would be sold to someone who was, so the problem of locating the borrower was not serious. He would not be let off the ship until he could be turned over to someone with a financial interest in keeping track of him — in most cases, having him living under the same roof as a servant.

It has been estimated that more than half the white population of colonial America arrived as indentured servants.[8] Like every form of human activity, it had costs (including abuses) as well as benefits. The vast scale of the emigration paid by indentureship suggests that many found its benefits offsetting the costs, while they had the option. Government intervention, however, removed this option. The British government first forbade the emigration of artisans — who were much in demand in the United States — in 1788, and then in 1803 reduced the number of immigrants allowed per ship. This latter improvement on the quality of life aboard ship meant that the cost per passenger was raised to a level that made the transportation of indentured servants uneconomic.[9] Later, American social reformers' hostility to any form of contract labor found its way into laws and policies which removed this option.

ETHNIC BUSINESS

Businesses owned or operated by members of ethnic minorities can be divided into two broad categories: (1) those concentrating on selling to other members of the same ethnic group, and (2) those serving primarily the larger outside world. Virtually every American ethnic group has had some of both, but the amount and kind of entrepreneurship has varied greatly from one group to another.

As noted in chapter 3, discrimination in labor markets — whether antipathetic or perceptual discrimination — creates additional incentives for self-employment, including owner-operated businesses. Knowledge of the special consumer preferences of ethnic communities provides another incentive for ethnic businesses.

Ethnic Neighborhood Stores
Stores in ethnic neighborhoods may be run by members of the group dominating the neighborhood for any of a number of reasons. One would be simple proximity. Another would be familiarity and affinity with the local people. There may be special preferences — as for kosher food by Jews or a particular kind of clothing favored by Orientals. Sometimes it may be the atmosphere rather than the merchandise that attracts the particular group — a particular foreign language that is spoken or a given set of traditions or customs that are observed.

The extent to which an ethnic enclave creates a demand for stores and other businesses run by its own members varies from group to group and from good to good within a given group. Most groups do not care about the ethnicity of those who provide them with television programs, but do care who provides them with religious services. Even when the religion itself is the same — Catholicism for example — whether the priest is Irish, Polish, or Italian has been a matter of concern (and even insistence) by parishioners. Sometimes it is the larger society which determines that ethnic members wil perform certain services by default. The reluctance of whites to minister to the hair, the bodies, or the souls of blacks has created a class of black barbers, physicians, undertakers, and religious ministers.

The purely ethnic neighborhood store tends to lose its appeal over time, as the group acquires more generally "Americanized" tastes in both merchandise and atmosphere, and as the group becomes more geographically scattered. But even in an ethnic neighborhood that remains intact — as with many black ghettos, for example — most of the local stores may be owned by ethnically or racially different people. In short, the supply of entrepreneurship matters, as well as the demand for ethnic establishments.

Entrepreneurship varies greatly from group to group. It is commonplace among Jews, Armenians, Chinese, or Japanese, somewhat less common among the Irish, and rare among blacks. In Boston, around the turn of the century, the proportion of Jews who were business owners was nine times the proportion among the Irish.[10] In 1929, the payrolls of Oriental-owned businesses were about 35 times those of blacks, each group in relation to its proportion of the population.[11]

One ethnic group may supply the entrepreneurship needed to provide the goods desired by another ethnic group. As in other areas, intergroup harmony is neither necessary nor sufficient for economic transactions. Looked at another way, intergroup harmony is not a free good available in unlimited quantities. It must therefore be economized, like other scarce inputs. One particularly striking example may illustrate how Polish immigrants and Jewish immigrants in Chicago used to transact with a minimum of this scarce resource:

. . . the Poles and the Jews in Chicago . . . detest each other thoroughly, but they live side by side on the West side, and even more generally on the Northwest Side. They have a profound feeling of disrespect and contempt for each other, bred by their contiguity and by historical friction in the pale; but they trade with each other on Milwaukee Avenue and on Maxwell Street. A study of numerous cases shows that not only do many Jews open their businesses on Milwaukee Avenue and Division Street because they know that the Poles come from all over the city to trade on Maxwell Street but also because they know that there they can find the familiar street-stands owned by Jews. These two immigrant groups, having lived side by side in Poland and Galicia, are used to each other's business methods. They have accommodated themselves one to another, and this accommodation persists in America.[12]

Some have argued that the very different "representation" of various ethnic groups among business owners or managers reflect differing availabilities of capital needed to start a business, due to discrimination by banks. In fact, however, owner-operated businesses are seldom started with bank loans, regardless of the race or ethnicity of the businessman. The crucial information needed for assessing the prospects of an owner-operated business is information about the kind of person he is, and this information is much more readily available to the businessman's family and friends than to a bank. Where the risks of financing a given venture are different to one set of investors (the individual, his family or friends) than to another set of investors (banks and other distant financial institutions), then economic theory would predict that those investors with the least risk would be the ones to make the particular investment. Accordingly, we find most small businesses begin with capital supplied by the individual businessman and those closest to him.

The implications of this simple fact are many. For example, if banks are unable to sort good from bad risks as potential businessmen at a cost low enough to compete with family and friends, neither are other distant, formal institutions, such as government agencies set up to promote minority business. If the cost of knowledge is the crucial variable, then groups that are more close knit — i.e. where more individuals have intimate knowledge of each other's character — would be expected to have particularly large proportions of their people establish their own businesses, since they can draw on more people for capital. Both of these hypotheses are confirmed by the empirical evidence.

Groups with strong family and community ties — such as Chinese, Japanese, and Jews — have been prominent as entrepreneurs, setting up businesses with resources drawn from within the ethnic community, even during their early years in poverty. Jews often started as pushcart peddlers, Chinese as operators of tiny laundries, and Japanese and other such groups in similarly humble beginnings reflecting the small amount of capital initially available.

Blacks have seldom set up such businesses, but the particular subsets of blacks who have are revealing. Black West Indians, the Black Muslims, and the followers of Father Divine's religious sect have been very entrepreneurial.

Perhaps the most dramatic example of black entrepreneurial success was the last of these, with apparently some of the least promising prospects. Father Divine's religious sect set up hundreds of small businesses in the 1930s, during the worst depression in history, and among some of the poorest and least educated classes in the black community. The success of these ventures is in sharp contrast with the massive failures in the prosperous 1960s and 1970s of black businesses financed by the federal government in programs created by "experts", and often receiving preferential treatment by banks and private and governmental purchasers. The one advantage enjoyed by Father Divine — and by West Indians and Black Muslims — is that these were all groups separated from both black and white society, and intensely closely knit within themselves. They possessed the crucial human capital — knowledge of each other's character — necessary to raise financial capital, and to direct it to those individuals best able to put it to work successfully. The federal government programs had more capital but less knowledge — as their many disastrous investments indicated.

The same point has been made by saying that mutual trust has been the crucial ingredient in financing ethnic enterprises, for even relatively poor people can raise significant amounts of capital by pooling their individually meager resources.[13] However, "trust" by itself can be a prelude to disaster, as the fate of government minority business programs indicates, along with the history of black bank failures. It is true that the more successful groups, including subsets of blacks, have exhibted trust among themselves, but it is the knowledge behind the trust that is crucial — and the differential cost of personal knowledge among such people that makes the trust possible and successful

Ethnic Businesses with Non-Ethnic Customers
Even businesses that began within an ethnic enclave have continued to expand only insofar as they could draw customers from the larger society. Jewish pushcart peddlars and tiny storeowners eventually graduated to owners of department stores and even chains of stores, serving a largely non-Jewish public. Macy's, Gimbels, and Bloomingdales are

as general in their clientele as any stores established by Anglo-Saxons. Japanese truck-farming long ago reached a scale going well beyond the level of sales in the Japanese-American community. Chinese, Italian, Greek, etc. restaurants serve their food to clientele not confined solely, or even mainly, to members of these respective groups.

The early history of black caterers in the United States followed a very similar pattern. When George Washington took his victorious officers to a farewell dinner after the American Revolutionary War, he took them to a tavern in New York owned by a black man. Black caterers in Philadelphia and in other cities in the nineteenth century were among the leading caterers of their time, serving a largely white (and wealthy) clientele. Such businesses were destroyed in the worsening racial atmosphere in northern cities around the turn of the century, as masses of uneducated, unacculturated blacks migrated to northern urban communities from the rural South. The polarization of the races cost black caterers their white clientele. Because the caterers were specialized to provide a service that only a relatively few wealthy whites could afford, the occupation was not viable as an enterprise serving the internal demands of the ethnic enclave.

HOUSING MARKETS

Densely crowded ethnic neighborhoods have existed as long as there has been migration to the cities, whether from the rural South or from rural backgrounds in Europe. Many of the other housing phenomena of today's ghettos can be found among the Irish in the early nineteenth century, among Jews toward the end of the century, or in many other groups at various times and places. Several patterns have emerged repeatedly with the mass movement of racial or ethnic groups into the cities:

1 The abandonment of whole neighborhoods by others as the new ethnic group begins to move in.

2 Increasing density of people per unit of housing space, often accomplished by subdividing houses into apartments, or large apartments into smaller apartments.

3 A decline in the amount of maintenance of buildings by landlords.

4 A deterioration in community standards of sanitation.

These phenomena were common with the Irish or the Jews in the nineteenth century, or with blacks or Puerto Ricans in the twentieth century. Does this pattern represent discrimination (antipathetic or perceptual), or a generally accurate assessment of the effect of particular groups of people on the physical property or the tranquility and safety of other people? What matters analytically is not which theory seems more plausible initially, but how their respective implications can be deduced in such a way as to confront empirical evidence.

Housing Segregation
Insofar as group antipathy is involved, one would expect longer-lasting and more pervasive residential segregation than if merely perceptual discrimination were involved. Groups easily identifiable, whether by dress or skin color, would face the more long-lasting discrimination. Insofar as mere "stereotypes" based on ignorance were responsible for intergroup segregation or friction, one should not expect to find the same residential separation *within* the affected group as *between* that group and the larger society. The far greater knowledge of a group that exists within that group would preclude internal residential segregation based on ignorance — *if* perceptual discrimination explained housing patterns.

Insofar as the residential separation reflects accurate knowledge of intergroup differences, entirely different phenomena should be observed:

1 Similar residential separation patterns within as between groups, since the causes of separation are actual differences of behavior and values, rather than misperceptions. Even if the larger society does not perceive *intra*group

differences, members of the group itself will, and will therefore create internal residential segregation.

2 Changing residential separation patterns between groups over time — less segregation when acculturation reduces intergroup differences, and increased segregation when those differences are accentuated, as by the in-migration of less acculturated members of the segregated group.

3 Intergroup differences not attributable to discrimination should be as apparent as differences attributable to discrimination. If, by hypothesis, there are real intergroup differences causing the residential separation, then evidences of this should appear in matters independent of majority volition — for example, rates of drunkenness or disease among the groups segregated.

Historically, virtually all groups have been residentially concentrated to one degree or another, for a longer or shorter span of time. In other words, there has never been a random distribution of people by ethnicity, even holding income constant. For example, even today "51.6 per cent of the population of Southern European origin would have to be redistributed in order to achieve full integration with the Northern European population . . . [14] This residential segregation simply happens not to be visible to the naked eye because the people are all the same color, but it is no less real. The housing segregation index for Puerto Ricans — most of whom are white — is the same as that for blacks. [15] In short, specifically *racial* residential segregation is not unique, except in its visibility.

The social phenomenon today known as "white flight" was common long before there were color differences involved. When Irish immigrants moved into nineteenth-century neighborhoods, the original inhabitants fled. [16] Indeed, middle-class blacks fled Detroit neighborhoods into which Polish immigrants moved in the nineteenth century. [17] There was the same reaction to successive streams of other immigrants, and to black migrants from the rural South. Nor were the group differences imaginary. When a cholera epidemic went through Boston in the 1840s, it went almost exclusively through Irish neighborhoods.[18] Clearly this was not volitional discrimination. It reflected different standards of sanitation in such neighborhoods, which made them vulnerable to a plague that not only spared other neighborhoods, but which had spared all of Boston before the Irish immigrants came. A similar pattern existed with other diseases and other cities.[19] In short, objective evidence confirms contemporary observations that the residentially separated group was indeed different in its behavior, in ways that imposed numerous costs on their neighbors.

The point is not to "blame" the Irish or others. Virtually every ethnic group from a rural background has taken generations to become habituated to the requirements of urban sanitation. It was not that it was *intellectually* difficult to trace the relationship between uncovered garbage and a large rat population. What was difficult was for a whole group to become so *habituated* to using covered garbage cans as to make a large rat population impossible. Even if *most* people carefully disposed of their garbage, as long as a substantial minority did not, the neighborhood would sustain a large rat population and the diseases they carried. The intellectual simplicity of this in no way implies that such behavior would become habitual before the passage of many years. More typically, it would take generations. In the meantime, others tended to put distance between themselves and those whose presence meant increased disease, noise, and violence.

Group separation under these conditions is not merely a redistribution of given amounts of costs and benefits. Insofar as it takes only a significant minority of people to make a given neighborhood overrun with rats, or to make schools too disorderly for education, the random diffusion of such people throughout a city can mean a larger total number of neighborhoods infested with rats and a larger total number of schools where education is impossible. Where groups are sorted out by ethnicity, the biggest losers are those members of the excluded group who do not create social costs but who must pay the penalty for those who do. Were such groups randomly distributed, such people would gain but other people would lose — and the losses and gains would not cancel out if there were more total costs, whether measured in rats and disease, or violence and lost education. Again, it must be noted that people who pay costs are no less important if they do not belong to an identifiable ethnic group.

Most ethnic neighborhoods have been much more minutely divided than by such gross group designations as "Jews", "the Irish", etc. For example, the lower east side of New York in the nineteenth century was not simply a Jewish neighborhood. Roumanian Jews lived in a different section from Polish Jews and Bohemian Jews elsewhere. Among Italians, the neighborhood concentrations in America typically followed the village or province from which they had come in Italy. There was no random residential distribution within the ethnic enclave, any more than between the ethnic enclave and the larger society. To the larger society all Jews or Italians might "look alike", so these intra-ethnic concentrations undermine the view that residential segregation is evidence of the larger society's actions. When the same phenomenon occurs where the larger society lacks the knowledge to discriminate (so minutely), the presence of the phenomenon where discrimination is possible does not imply that discrimination must be the cause.

The residential segregation of blacks in northern cities has typically been greater than the residential segregation of any given white ethnic group. However, in nineteenth-century America, the segregation of native stock Americans from immigrants as a group was virtually as complete. Moreover, the historical pattern of black segregation in northern cities is revealing as to causation.

The massive black ghettos that had become common in major northern cities by the middle of the twentieth century were largely a post-World War I development. As of about 1910 in Chicago, for example, more than two-thirds of the black population lived in neighborhoods where the majority of the residents were white.[20] In 1860 Detroit, 80 per cent of the black population lived in "a small contiguous area", but even within that area there was no racial segregation of the sort that became common later, for "no street in the city was even 50 per cent black occupied".[21] Similarly in New York at the turn of the twentieth century, there were "sections of Negro concentration" but "no single large neighborhood was an all-Negro community".[22] W. E. B. DuBois' descriptions of late nineteenth-century Philadelphia suggest something similar.[23] In the nation's capital at about the same time there were no "clear-cut solid black belts . . . outside of which Negroes could not find housing", and though such patterns later developed, there was "some intersprinkling of white and Negro dwellings" on into the 1930s.[24]

Most of the black urban communities of the north began well before the Civil War, peopled by blacks born free in the north, others escaped from slavery in the South, or "free persons of color" who migrated from the South. These tiny communities were similar to concentrations of various European ethnic groups in that people neither were randomly distributed about the city nor exclusively dominated a given neighborhood. Blacks, however, were denied many of the political rights and access to public accommodations open to others. With the passage of time, however, these legal disabilities and bars to public places tended to disappear in northern cities, even though (1) blacks remained an insignificant proportion of the voters, and (2) there was no pressure in this direction from the judiciary or the federal government. In short, white public and political opinion changed over a period of decades in the nineteenth-century northern urban centers.

DuBois wrote of nineteenth-century Philadelphia, "living men can remember when a Negro could not sit in a street car or walk many streets in peace". He said, "These times have passed, however", in 1899, and pointed to greater access to hotels, restaurants, theaters, etc.[25] There was in DuBois' words, "a growing liberal spirit toward the Negro in Philadelphia" in which "the community was disposed to throw off the trammels, brush away petty hindrances and to soften the harshness of race prejudice" — one consequence of which was a "greater freedom of domicile which has since come . . . ".[26] Similar trends were emerging in other northern cities around the country at the same time. Jacob Riis found this in New York.[27] In Detroit, blacks who had been denied the vote in 1850 were voting in the 1880s, and access to public accommodations was also increasing.[28] Detroit's black upper class at this point had "interaction with whites on a regular and equal basis" — having attended high school and college in an integrated setting.[29] Black physicians and dentists "had mostly white practices",[30] and in politics there was a "regular election of black men to public office in Michigan in the 1890s . . . ".[31] In Illinois by 1885 there was "a public opinion strong enough to erase all of the discrimination laws from the state's statute book", even though blacks lacked political power themselves and simply appealed to the general electorate on the basis of principles.[32] In Chicago at this time "there was considerable social intercourse between colored and white people, and marriages across the color-line were not unknown".[33] More generally, Chicago blacks were in this era "accepted as a normal part of the city's life".[34] Throughout the north "an unprecedented period of racial amity and integration was prevailing, especially between 1870 and 1890".[35]

This brief and promising era of improving race relations was followed, in most northern cities, by increased hostility, violence, discrimination — and housing segregation. In short, the changing pattern of residential concentration over time paralleled more general trends in intergroup relations. The general trends from mid-nineteenth-century hostility to blacks, to end-of-the-century growing acceptance, to more segregation and discrimination are hard to reconcile with purely "racist" explanations, unless these were simply inexplicable "swings of the pendulum" in white public opinion. These trends are, however, consistent with other evidence that there were, in fact, changing characteristics of the black population itself in northern cities.

Like many other ethnic groups from a rural background arriving in an urban society and a commercial and industrial economy, blacks went through a period of adjustment, complicated by the arrival of new waves of unacculturated compatriots. The timing and size of these new waves have proven crucial for the prospects of blacks as a group, as they have for Italians, Jews, and others. Where relatively small increments of newcomers are absorbed into the existing ethnic community, the dominant economic and social pattern of the group as a whole is its progressive adaptation to the urban economy and society — not only objectively, but also in the perceptions of the larger surrounding society.

At the beginning of the nineteenth century, there was much optimism about northern blacks and whites coexisting amicably.[36] However, growing persecution of "free persons of color" in the South[37] forced many free Negroes "in the rough" to migrate from the region and move into northern cities, where — like many other unacculturated elements in other ethnic groups — they became disproportionately represented among paupers, vagrants, and criminals.[38] Thus began a "radical opposition to the Negro",[39] spreading through all of white society — the first of many retrogressions in race relations brought on by similar events. It was a "steady forcing down of the status of the Free Negro in all parts of the country".[40]

As the newcomers "in the rough" became, over the years, part of a more acculturated black community, the color barriers began coming down again, in the manner already noted. But this was not a mere happenstance in the history of white public opinion in a vacuum. By contemporary accounts, the northern black communities themselves were becoming more safe, self-supporting, clean, etc. Jacob Riis in the 1890s noted "a distinct and gratifying improvement" among the blacks in New York City, declaring that there was "no more clean and orderly community in New York . . . ".[41] DuBois likewise found among Philadelphia Negroes at the same time a "distinct improvement in their family life during the last quarter century".[42] A modern historian has noted that blacks in New York at this point were "better off than the mass of recent white immigrants".[43] Black waiters received higher pay than Irish waiters in New York's restaurants and black workers helping to build New York's Croton reservoir received higher pay than Italian workers on the same project.[44] DuBois noted similar progress in Philadelphia, where black waiters and cooks had graduated into the ranks of some of the leading caterers in the city "who amassed fortunes for themselves and won general respect for their people".[45]

There seemed to be ample ground for optimism about the

future of race relations in the north as the twentieth century began — just as there had seemed to be at the beginning of the nineteenth century. In both cases, these hopes were destroyed by events in the South. Jim Crow laws and mob violence in the South provoked a new wave of black migration — larger than ever before — to northern urban centers. The demand for more workers in northern factories during World War I added to the massive migration, which doubled or tripled from one decade to the next. The consequences were another massive setback in race relations generally, and the hardening of residential housing segregation in particular. Many contemporary northern blacks openly blamed the Southern migrants for the retrogression which now afflicted blacks as a group.[46] The hardening of class lines within the black community at the same time[47] further supports the hypothesis that the characteristics of the northern black urban population were in fact changing. Writing in the midst of the massive black migration out of the South, a distinguished black historian predicted: "The maltreatment of the Negro will be nationalized by this exodus".[48]

Product Quality
Housing, like all other products, varies in quality. As might be expected, on the simplest economic principles, the higher quality housing has generally been occupied by higher income people and lower quality housing by lower income people. This has been true not only as of a given time, but also over time: as the real wealth created by the economy has risen, so has the average housing quality.

These extremely elementary economic propositions must be stated and insisted upon at the outset, because a large literature proceeds as if housing quality were primarily a function of morality or political policy so that rents are determined by "greedy" landlords, slums by "heartless" investors or "public neglect", and in turn become "nurseries of crime" among those who grow up in them.[49] Moreover, the long continuum of housing quality — extending from mansions to hovels — has been dichotomized into (1) something called "decent" housing, and (2) housing failing to meet this opaque but imperative standard. Thus, a leading historian writes "the problem of finding decent working-class housing was never solved".[50] The only empirical meaning of such statements seems to be that the quality of housing which middle-class writers are used to is higher than the quality of housing working-class people live in — an unsurprising result, which conveys more information about the egocentricity of middle-class writers than about housing.

Because most urban ethnic groups have, at some period or other, lived primarily in lower than average quality housing — in "slums" — the egocentric conceptions of middle-class observers have been of more than theoretical interest. Through much of the nineteenth century, discussions of slums were discussions of ethnic neighborhoods, because virtually no native born Americans were to be found in the urban slums. There were many journalistic exposés of slum conditions in the nineteenth and early twentieth centuries, and political crusades led by middle-class people, aimed at getting government to reduce housing options through "slum clearance" or laws outlawing the building of "substandard" housing. Particularly in the nineteenth and early twentieth centuries, "slum clearance" or the prevention of the building of certain kinds of housing were the main thrust of such "reform" efforts — i.e. pure reduction of options. Today there is also some emphasis on *creating* options by building government-financed housing for the poor. Nevertheless, even today, the government destroys more low-income housing than it builds. On net balance, today's policies, like those of the past, end up reducing the housing options of low-income people (see the detailed discussion below). Those unfamiliar with economic analysis using indifference curves may skip to page 77.

This process can be analyzed with the help of traditional economic analysis (see figure 4.2). The total amount of goods available have been divided into housing and non-housing. Housing may be conceived of in purely quantitative terms (floorspace per person, for example) or as some quantitative equivalent of increasing quality. It does not matter which, for this particular analysis. The line B_pB_p is the budget constraint line of the poor. The highest level of consumer satisfaction achievable within this constraint is indifference curve I_2, where the poor have H_p in housing and N_p in non-housing goods. The budget constraint line of the middle class ($B_m B_m$) permits a higher level of satisfaction, on indifference curve I_5, where the middle class consumes N_m in non-housing goods and H_m in housing. Among the non-housing goods desired by the middle class is observation of better housing inhabited by the poor. That is, middle-class people would be on a still higher indifference curve (I_6) if they were not saddened by seeing the poor living in slums. The budget line $B'_m B_m$ indicates the higher range of options possible for the middle class if the poor were better housed.

Somewhere between the housing to which the middle-class individual is accustomed (H_m) and the housing of the poor individual (H_p) lies the boundary of "decent" housing, as conceived by the middle class. Insofar as middle-class reform efforts (slum clearance, building codes, housing regulations, etc.) are successful, all housing less than this will become illegal. Once this option-

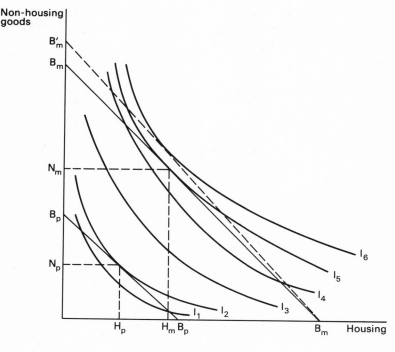

FIGURE 4.2

reduction has occurred, either all housing choices to the left of H_d in figure 4.3 will disappear (with perfect law enforcement at zero cost), or will become more costly to the extent that inspectors, policemen, or politicians must be bribed to overlook violations, or to the extent that tenants run higher risks of being summarily evicted when the property is officially condemned, at the insistence of their middle-class benefactors. These costs will of course be greater, the further the particular housing falls below the legally prescribed standard of "decent housing" (since the size of the bribe is limited by the cost of correcting the violations). The shaded area of figure 4.3 shows these additional costs of "substandard" housing after it has been declared illegal. The net result is that those poor who live in substandard housing must sacrifice more non-housing goods to supply their housing requirements. The new budget constraint line of the poor is $B'_p B_p$. Their new equilibrium must fall below their initial level of satisfaction on indifference curve I_2, given that H_d is between H_p and H_m — that being the empirical meaning of "decent housing".

Some subsidiary implications of this analysis may be worth noting. Insofar as the ownership and management of substandard housing entails the bribery of officials after housing reform, those individuals with moral scruples would tend to avoid becoming

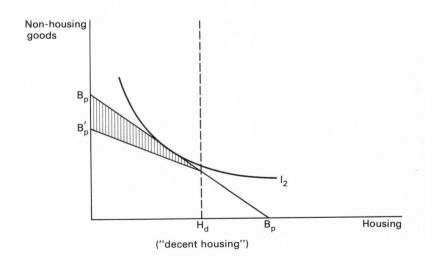

FIGURE 4.3

owners or managers of such property. Looked at another way, the average moral quality of landlords to the poor tends to decline. Insofar as there is some minimum level of bribe for which an inspector, policeman, or politician would jeopardize himself, there would not be a smoothly widening band of additional costs to substandard housing, as depicted in figure 4.3. Rather, all housing whose fix-up costs were less than the minimum bribery requirement would be fixed up instead — providing middle-class reformers with "proof" that their reforms were "working" and only needed to be pushed with more zeal.

Economic analysis thus leads to the conclusion that (1) the poor end up on a lower indifference curve, with better housing and less non-housing goods, while (2) the middle-class end up on a higher indifference curve, with at least more non-housing goods and perhaps more housing as well, depending upon the particular nature of income and substitution effects. While there has been no direct money transfer between the poor and the middle class in this example, movements from one indifference curve to another are changes in real income. There has been an increase in the real income of the middle class caused by a reduction in the real income of the poor. The economic effect is the same as if there had been a direct transfer. Social justifications of transfers from lower income groups to higher income groups are difficult, and no such justification will be attempted here.

To what extent is empirical evidence consistent with these theoretical conclusions? Politically, in cities around the country, people in ethnic slums consistently voted *against* reformers who favored slum clearance and numerous other "humane" reductions in their options in other aspects of life. Where zoning laws are put to a referendum, the middle class support them and the poor oppose them. Even Jacob Riis, a turn-of-the-century reform zealot, noted that in the slums "owner and tenant alike" objected to housing regulations and slum clearance, and often "the police had to drag tenants out by force"[51] from condemned dwellings. This was not said in any way suggesting a reconsideration of his reforming passion, but as a curious observation on the perversity of lesser beings.

Knowledge cost differentials may explain the perennial middle-class preference for a higher standard of housing for the poor than the poor choose to inhabit (a re-phrasing of the proposition that "the problem of finding decent working-class housing was never solved"). The poor directly experience both their housing and their non-housing consumption, and so have knowledge of both at zero cost, and automatically develop their own sense of trade-off. The middle class can only observe the poor, and so have positive knowledge costs. Moreover, these knowledge costs vary from one good to another, being cheapest for the housing which the poor inhabit (which is visible to all), and most expensive for other things and particularly for the subjective trade-off rate (the shape of the indifference curve) of the poor, which is inside their brains and could be inferred only from close observation of their revealed preferences — i.e. at substantial cost.

Lack of knowledge can be dealt with in many ways, but it must be recognized before it can be dealt with at all. Seldom does a more affluent class with more years of formal schooling seriously consider the possibility that they may be less informed than a poorer class with less formal schooling. Moreover, the general progress of the economy typically increases the real income of the poor over time, and these rising budget constraint lines typically mean more and better housing over time — a result which can then be seen by reform-minded people as proof of the success of their political efforts.

An empirical test of the effect of housing reform efforts might be a comparison of housing quality over time in two areas — both subject to rising incomes, but only one subject to significant housing reform efforts or housing reform laws. During the hey-day of housing reform efforts in the northern ethnic slums — the period roughly from the Civil War to World War I — nothing at all comparable was being said or done politically about the housing of the newly freed blacks in the rural South. Newly freed blacks generally lived in the same kind of housing they had lived in as slaves — log cabins with dirt floors and no plumbing or windowpanes. With the passage of time, however, log cabins were replaced by plank houses, and windowpanes began to appear. This happened not only where blacks owned their homes, but where the houses were supplied by white landowners to black sharecroppers. Contrary to the volitional theory of pricing, competition forced landowners to increase their sharecroppers' incomes as technology and the sharecroppers' human capital both improved over time. A part of the sharecroppers' income was in kind — notably housing. Those landlords who replaced log cabins with plank houses acquired a competitive advantage in recruiting sharecroppers, and, once that became common, those who installed windowpanes acquired another advantage in having numerous applicants to be sharecroppers, permitting a selection of the most desirable workers. Through ordinary economic processes, the kind of housing that blacks occupied immediately after the Civil War had almost entirely disappeared by the turn of the century[52] — without any of the "slum clearance" or other housing crusades found in the north during the same era. The reformer's view that his efforts were what produced housing improvement is reminiscent of the story of the rooster who thought that it was his conscientious crowing and vigorous flapping of wings that caused the sun to rise.

Product Prices

Even people who recognize the effect of supply and demand on prices (and product quality) in general, nevertheless often proceed on the basis of a volitional theory of pricing in the case of housing and labor — the landlord or employer being able to impose whatever terms he chooses, and therefore being morally liable as well as causally responsible for high rents or low wages. This belief usually survives as an unarticulated premise, for if articulated it would have to confront the existence of far more landlords and employers than is consistent with theories of collusive or monopolistic behavior. Empirically, it would have to confront the even more difficult fact that, in the hey-day of low-paid "sweatshop" labor in the ethnic ghettos of nineteenth-century New York, the owners of sweatshops made low profits[53] — even though they themselves worked long hours — suggesting that "exploitation" was hardly the explanation of low wages.

In the case of housing, pricing is somewhat more complicated. In slum housing especially, the prices *charged* were not always synonymous with the prices *paid*, since slum dwellers of whatever ethnicity have long had records of non-payment of rent, both willfully and through unemployment or other misfortunes. There were 11,000 evictions in just two judicial districts on the lower east side of New York in 1891-92. [54] Records of rents charged are misleading evidence on the income of rental property, given that the property is not continuously fully rented, nor continuously paid for when it is rented. The deduction of capital losses due to tenant damages (including sporadic fires destroying the whole property) further complicate the calculation of net profit. In the hey-day of overcrowded slums in nineteenth century New York, when "the greed of capital" was blamed, contemporary hearings indicated "net profits of 6-15 per cent" on slum housing. [55] Yet reformers clearly believed in the theory of volitional pricing by the landlord: "It is a plain question of the percent he is willing to take". [56]

Evidence for the belief that landlords were charging "too much" consisted of a comparison with contemporary model tenements financed by philanthropic middle-class investors who limited their return to 3 or 5 per cent. [57] These model tenements were rented to "selected tenants as to trustworthiness and desirability" [58] (and higher occupations than slum dwellers [59]). The model tenements were located "an hour's journey" [60] from downtown Manhattan. Yet this experience was generalized to the very different question of housing *within walking distance of their jobs* for an *unselected mass* of recent immigrants with lower occupational status — people shown by the reformers' own research to exhibit great amounts of violence, drunkenness, dirt, disease, etc., [61] to a far greater extent than, say, black ghettos today.

Again, with the passage of time, new options were created by the economy — notably the spread of subways and electric trolleys, which permitted the people packed into the slums to spread out over wider spaces, and still be able to get to work. Other economic advances, not so directly linked to housing patterns, nevertheless created the wealth that allowed slum dwellers to choose higher quality housing that they could now afford. The gradual acculturation of the nineteenth-century immigrants likewise raised their tastes and lowered their rates of crime and disease. Many of their descendants now live in middle-class suburbs and often wonder how black or Hispanic ghettos can be so terrible, when in fact those of their ancestors were far worse.

When the lower east side of New York was a Jewish slum, it contained three times as many people per square mile as it does today. [62] Half slept three or four to a room, and nearly 25 per cent slept five to a room. [63] The murder rate in mid-nineteenth-century Boston was three times what it was in the middle of the twentieth century. [64] All the ghetto riots of the 1960s combined did not kill as many people as were killed in one Irish riot in 1863. [65] As for substandard housing, mid-nineteenth-century slums had toilets in the yards and alleys behind the buildings. [66] Only later in the century did running water come into the buildings themselves, to be *shared* by the tenants, both at faucets and in toilets. In 1894 there were only 51 private toilets in nearly 4,000 tenements and only 306 persons out of more than a quarter of a million had bathtubs in their homes. [67]

The fact that profits were not unusually high on either the slum dwellings, nor from the employment of slum workers, suggests that such accommodations were all that could be produced at a cost within the range of their own productivity. Inherent constraints are not as exciting as sin, but they are more central to economics.

IMPLICATIONS

Throughout the range of consumer purchases — from ocean voyages to rental housing — ethnic minorities have at one time or other either received products of appalling quality or paid above-average prices, or sometimes both. Usually these things happened in highly competitive markets, where economic theory would lead us to expect that excess profits would attract entry, leading to the competing away of any especially lucrative "exploitation". Empirically, such data as are available indicate no unusual profit rates, nor any that would have permitted significantly lower prices or higher quality, even if investors had accepted a zero rate of return.

The fact that many supermarkets are moving *out* of today's ghetto neighborhoods suggests that the high prices there are not producing high profits, but reflect higher costs. While much of the historical, sociological, or journalistic literature has long regarded lower income ethnic groups as ignorant or irrational dupes, taken advantage of by "exploiters", there has been too much consistency in their behavior — whether as consumers or voters — to attribute it to anything as random as irrationality. The preferences of low-income ethnic groups have simply differed from the preferences of middle-class observers, less familiar with the full range of parameters affecting their behavior. That such a noted reformer as Jacob Riis could ignore poor people's need to walk to work (in the era before subways or automobiles) was typical of middle-class reformers' outlooks, which caused nineteenth-century ethnic minorities to be consistently opposed to them politically, and to evade their laws and policies wherever possible. Reformers' attempts to benefit such ethnic groups have frequently taken the form of reducing their options, thereby lowering their real income.

CHAPTER FIVE

The Economics of Slavery

No account of ethnicity in America is complete without considering the unique experience of blacks as slaves for two centuries. This is not only historically important, but has implications for present-day controversies over such issues as "compensation" for past injustices. Moreover, slavery is an important economic phenomenon in itself, and one in which the degree to which markets were allowed to function had major effects on blacks and on the larger society.

Slavery has existed for thousands of years, on every continent, with numerous modifications, and encompassing a remarkable range of occupations. Most slaves in the antebellum South worked on cotton plantations, but some were urban slaves, including many skilled artisans. The range even extended to a riverboat captain commanding a crew that included white sailors.[1] In Greek and Roman antiquity, slave occupations extended from the lowliest work to teachers, doctors, and managers of imperial estates.[2]

As with other complex social phenomena, economic analysis can begin with the simplest, most skeletal, features of slavery, and later consider the flesh and blood of historical reality in its complexities and inconsistencies.

PURE SLAVERY

By a pure slave system is meant slavery unmodified by any of the admixtures of other economic institutions which sometimes changed the master-slave relationship in the direction of an employer—employee relationship, or some other economic mode. In an unmodified slave system, work is accomplished on orders from hierarchical superiors, culminating in the slave owner, and the worker's incentive is avoidance of punishment. After considering the economic consequences of this method of production, we can then proceed to consider why and in what kinds of conditions it was modified, sometimes drastically. These modifications indicate the areas of slavery's economic disadvantages, and suggest some of the reasons for particular features of other economic systems.

Security Costs
The first requirement for the existence of slavery as a system is some method of restricting escape, rebellion, sabotage, or other actions which could render the system impossible or unprofitable. This does not mean that there must be *none* of these things. All have occurred in slave systems around the world and down through history. Slave systems, however, perpetuate themselves by making incremental trade-offs between the costs incurred in restricting escape and resistance, and the costs which such escapes and resistance would entail. For example, chaining all slaves together would reduce escapes, but would also reduce work efficiency, and was seldom (if ever) done on antebellum slave plantations in the South. Slave traders might use such methods for slaves in transit or awaiting sale, but in these circumstances there were no opportunity costs in foregone output. High fences and a corps of armed guards would reduce escapes, but this approach was also seldom (if ever) used on Southern slave plantations, because of its cost. In short, slavery's basic requirement of reducing escape and resistance had not simply to be met, but met in economically efficient ways.

Among the costs of restricting escape was a limitation on the kinds of work performed by those slaves who worked under a system of pure or unalloyed slavery. Such slaves were not used in tasks requiring wide dispersion or extensive travel, both of which would present obvious escape opportunities. Neither were they used in work requiring firearms or control of large sums of money, both of which can be used to facilitate escape.

Far cheaper than chains, fences, and armed guards was simple ignorance as a method of preventing escape and resistance. Slaves were kept illiterate by most slave owners in the antebellum South, and the law made this legally mandatory. Even if some particular slave owner might find it unnecessary, or not cost-effective, to keep his own slaves illiterate, the ease with which literacy can be spread would have meant large external costs to other slave owners and to slavery as a system if literacy became widespread among a slave population which engaged in inter-plantation visits.

One consequence of relying on ignorance rather than fences or guards was that it was relatively easy for slaves to escape temporarily from plantations in the South, but very difficult to escape permanently. There was enough temporary running away of slaves to create a market for people and dogs who specialized in tracking down the escapees. Permanent escape required finding a way out of the South, through hundreds of miles of unknown territory and hostile populations who could spot the escapee very easily by his skin color. For someone with no ability to read, much less read a map, it was a nearly impossible task. Permanent escape was more of a possibility for those few isolated individuals who had somehow acquired literacy, or who had access to the knowledge of others who operated the "underground railroad" network that helped thousands of slaves escape to the north. Significantly, most of the slaves who escaped through the "underground railroad" came from within a hundred miles of some free state. Over all, only about one out of every two thousand antebellum slaves escaped permanently.[3]

Illiteracy reduced the incentive to escape as well as virtually eliminating the means. People whose whole universe was reduced by illiteracy to their own personal experience and unreliable folklore would be more readily induced to regard slavery as inevitable. Literacy would have permitted slaves to become more valuable to slave owners by the increased range of work they could have performed, but it would also have given the slaves access to pictures of the possibilities and meaning of freedom, as well as increased chances of achieving it. The literacy of slaves was therefore regarded as a prime danger to be guarded against in the antebellum South.

Indeed, the literacy of *free* blacks — and in fact, their very presence — raised the cost of holding slaves. The literacy of "free persons of color" could readily spread to slaves, with whom they had social contacts, and therefore many Southern states not only refused to educate free Negroes but made it a crime for them even to attend private schools at their own expense.

In addition to simple ignorance, inducing such psychological traits as resignation, dependency, and awe of whites, were other low-cost devices used to reduce escapes and resistance. For these, too, the presence of "free persons of color" raised the cost of slavery. Laws forced free Negroes into publicly subservient behavior toward all whites — for example, requiring them to step aside or even get off the sidewalk for white pedestrians. Other laws created numerous economic, social, and legal difficulties for them, giving them incentives to leave areas where there were slave plantations.

While these laws have often been viewed as simple "racism" — a consumer good for bigots — the particular pattern of regional variations in the severity of such laws and practices suggests that they were also (and perhaps primarily) an *investment* good for reducing slave escapes or resistance. The laws and practices against "free persons of color" were almost invariably most severe in those states, and regions within states, where plantation slavery was concentrated.[4] With respect to time, they were most severe after slave uprisings.[5]

Such laws made freedom less enticing, since it was not complete freedom for blacks, as well as removing a possible source of accessories in achieving it. As a result of the intolerable conditions such laws created, many "free persons of color" migrated away from slave concentrations. The migration patterns of "free persons of color" were the opposite of the migration patterns of slaves. After the invention of the cotton gin near the end of the eighteenth century slaves in the nineteenth century were continually relocated from the upper South (notably Virginia) toward the cotton-growing lower South, especially a broad area known as "the black belt" stretching across Georgia, Alabama, Mississippi, Louisiana, and Arkansas. As the geographic center of the black population moved south-westward, at an average rate of about fifty miles per decade, the "free persons of color" moved in just the opposite direction — toward the upper South and the north — and within the South, away from rural plantation areas toward the cities. These destinations of "free persons of color" were all regions where there were either not as many repressive laws, or where the laws were not applied as stringently in practice. It would be hard to explain this pattern of variation in repressiveness on the basis of simple "racism" as a consumer good, though it fits completely the concept of an investment good for maintaining control of slaves.

While restrictions of the tasks, and of the mental and psychological development of slaves, were cheaper than purely physical methods of restraint, they were not free. Such economic constraints meant foregone opportunities for profit, because there were limits to the range of tasks that could be performed by people of given abilities, and limits to the range of abilities that could be permitted to be developed by people of a given potentiality.

The power of overseers or slave owners to humble or humiliate slaves for any reason or caprice meant that the pride and aspirations which serve as incentives in other economic systems were lacking under slavery, reducing individual initiative, trustworthiness, and other such intangible but valuable "human capital" inputs into economic processes. This disadvantage is common to systems of forced labor, ranging from prison labor to the military draft to serfdom. In all such systems, when particular tasks require initiative or trust, special modifications are introduced into the system to supplement the inadequate incentives provided by pure force.

While slavery restricted investments in the slave's *general* knowledge — which could facilitate his escape — it nevertheless provided incentives for investment in highly specific human capital among slaves. An ordinary employer's investment in the human capital of his employees is limited by the prospect of losing the return on that investment when they leave. The slave owner, however, has far less likelihood of losing the return on his investment in worker skills. Even if he later sells the slave, he can sell a skilled slave for a higher price. It is, therefore, not surprising to find skilled slave artisans common throughout the antebellum South. In some cases they worked at occupations from which blacks were later excluded after emancipation.

Some of the security costs of slave systems are "external costs",* paid by the free, non-slave-owning population — and some of these costs may last longer than slavery itself. Where a slave population is kept ignorant and psychologically repressed, and then emancipated, their later performance as free workers and members of the society may continue to cost the rest of the society directly (in increased public expenditures) or indirectly (in handicapped economic performance). During the period of slavery itself, there were costs externalized to Southern governments in activities such as special patrols to check slave passes and recapture escapees, or the temporary or permanent raising of police or military forces to guard against actual or anticipated slave rebellions. In the antebellum South there were also thought control efforts applied to the white population, to stifle any criticisms of slavery as an institution: abolitionist literature was even confiscated from the US mail by local authorities, and freedom of thought repressed at Southern colleges and universities, as well as in Southern newspapers, along with an atmosphere of extreme regionalism and hypersensitivity to criticism that drove out and kept out many individuals whose skills and talents would normally have benefitted the region. Some of these patterns and their economic consequences also lasted long past the Civil War, which intensified Southern regionalism.

In the twentieth century, decades of internal strife and violence in the South, centering around race and growing out

---

*Economists used the term "external costs" to refer to costs paid outside the decision-making unit that created them. The costs of air or water pollution are common examples.

of racial attitudes and practices originating under slavery, likewise made the South a less attractive place for outside capital, labor, or entrepreneurship. These instabilities and violence were deterrents to outsiders, quite aside from the merits of the various arguments involved, or any sympathies the outsiders may have had.

The extent to which such problems plagued the postbellum South in the nineteenth and twentieth centuries varied with the concentration of plantation slavery in the antebellum era. Those parts of the South particularly affected by lynchings, Ku Klux Klan activity, and other mob violence and political strife, were the "black belt" region of the deep South, which has long had the lowest average incomes among its white population. Conversely, the higher income, better educated, and otherwise more progressive regions within the South have been those which had the lowest concentration of slaves in the antebellum period, and the least use of slaves in the classic or pure plantation slavery system. The leading Southern universities are also concentrated in such regions. In short, slavery and its special security needs have had enduring external costs to the general white population of the South, most of whom owned no slaves.

Incentives for Slaves

Virtually unlimited punishment of slaves was legally permissible in most of the antebellum South. Even the death of a slave as a result of extreme punishment was unlikely to lead to serious criminal charges against the slave owner, much less a conviction by a local jury. Accordingly, punishments were in widespread use — but so too were numerous other incentives, including cash. When people with a virtually unlimited power of punishment resort to rewards to get certain work done, this implies some defect in punishment as an incentive system.

The effective imposition of punishment to achieve economic results requires some output norm which the worker must meet or exceed to escape the punishment. However, the high cost of knowledge of individual capabilities makes the setting of an optimal norm for slaves in general difficult, and the setting of different optimal norms for each individual virtually impossible. Slavery is the extreme limit of a more general decision-making problem when *power* is concentrated in one group of people and the relevant *knowledge* is concentrated in another. Individual slaves know what they can do, better than an overseer or slave owner knows, but under pure slavery they have no incentive to convey that knowledge, and in many cases considerable incentives to hide or understate it.

A similar problem exists in centrally planned economies, where the planning authority holds the power but the individual plant and farm managers have the knowledge as to what can and cannot be achieved with their own respective equipment and labor forces. In both cases (slavery and central planning) the power-holders may resort to pay incentives — special bonuses for exceeding established norms — in order to get individuals with above-average potential to reveal it, and in hopes of getting all concerned to strive more, thereby in effect selling their secrets for bonus money. In both systems, those tempted by rewards also know that increased production can mean higher norms set later, so that future economic rewards will be reduced as future demands on them are increased. This is one of the reasons why labor unions oppose piecework, and why outstanding workers are likely to be unpopular with fellow-workers under any economic system.

The separation of power and knowledge under slavery was dealt with not only by creating financial incentives (moving out of the realm of pure slavery), but also by selecting work which could be monitored cheaply and in which individual worker variations were of less importance. Routine manual labor on a mass production pattern fitted these requirements, and cotton growing and picking was the principal example in the antebellum South, where about 60 per cent of all slaves were employed in cotton production. Here was the extreme of pure slavery, with field hands working under the direct supervision and scrutiny of slave drivers and overseers with whips. Many other kinds of work were also performed by slaves in the antebellum South (and in other slave systems), and for those kinds of work where the knowledge-power separation was important, slavery was modified to encompass a wider range of incentives.

Incentives for Overseers and Slave Owners

Slave overseers had incentives to maximize output over the time span of their tenure, irrespective of the longer-run costs in terms of prematurely worn-out workers, exhaustion of the soil, or poor maintenance of barns, fences, and other farm equipment. Such incentives are particularly strong where overseers are paid a percentage of the value of each current crop. But the incentives for short-run maximization are not wholly absent even when overseers are salaried, for their past performance is the major determinant of future demand for their services by slave owners. There are very different costs of knowledge in assessing different parts of their performance. Their achievements are more readily measured in output per acre (or per worker) than in some indefinite estimate of long-run damage to workers or capital.

The slave owner's incentive is to maximize the long-run output of his land, capital, and slaves — which is to say, to maximize their present value. The economic conflict of his incentives with the short-run maximization incentives of overseers is reflected in (1) the fact that in slave owner's written instructions to overseers their "initial topic was usually the care of the slaves",[6] (2) firing of overseers for abuse of slaves,[7] and (3) a difference between the care and maintenance of both slaves and the plantation itself when the slave owner was living on the land than when he was a distant absentee owner leaving control in the hands of an overseer. Absentee ownership meant more overworked slaves and rundown plantations.

The extremes to which this could be carried were illustrated by the slave plantations in the British West Indies, whose owners typically lived in London. Infant mortality among slave women in the West Indies was several times what it was among slave women in the antebellum South, where most slave owners lived on their land. To a slave overseer, an infant had no economic value that would be realized during his tenure, so his incentive was to continue extracting labor from the pregnant woman, past the point where it imperilled the survival of the unborn infant. Ignorance compounded the effect of these incentives. Most slave overseers in the West Indies were bachelors, whereas plantation owners in the antebellum South typically had wives, who assumed responsibility for pregnant slave women. The economic output of the unborn infant was part of the present value of the slave owning family's estate. As one historian of slavery put it, "while crops were merely income, slaves were capital". [8]

Other risks to slaves were likewise risks to the present value of the slave owner's assets. Slaves cost from a thousand to two thousand dollars each (at nineteenth-century price levels), and so represented a substantial investment. Accordingly, slave owners often hired free workers to do hazardous work, rather than use their own slaves. A northern visitor in the antebellum South was surprised to find slaves throwing 500-pound bales of cotton down a ramp to Irish workmen on a river boat, who had the hazardous job of catching the heavy bales. He was told: "The niggers are worth too much to be risked here; if the Paddies are knocked over board, or get their backs broke, nobody loses anything". [9] It was a common practice in the South to hire Irishmen for work considered too dangerous for slaves — draining swamps that might be malarial, [10] cutting down trees that might fall on someone, [11] building levees that might collapse on the workmen, [12] facing the numerous hazards of building railroads, [13] or tending a steamboat's boiler that might blow up. [14] Particularly after slave prices rose in the early nineteenth century, "slaves were too precious for employment in any but the safest of tasks". [15] Economics forced a degree of consideration that humanitarianism had not.

The need to maintain slaves as capital likewise led to a level of food and housing comparable to that of contemporary white working people in the South, and a life expectancy greater than that of contemporary working class whites in the United States and Europe. [16] Slave cabins in the antebellum South were slightly larger, better ventilated, better heated, and somewhat more private than those of tenant farmers in contemporary Ireland. [17]

MODIFICATIONS OF SLAVERY

For tasks requiring individual initiative, discretion, and diligence, where close monitoring would be very costly, an alternative was to create better working conditions and incentive payments to elicit cooperation from slaves in return for some exemption from the rigors of pure slavery.

Tobacco manufacturing, for example, required much more initiative and discretion on the part of the individual worker, and slaves in the tobacco factories were treated quite differently from cotton field slaves. They were paid in cash, with bonuses for overtime, and were given cash allowances to buy their own food and rent living quarters that they selected for themselves in the local housing market. In short, their day-to-day lives were very much like those of any employees who live where they want, eat what they choose, and go back and forth between work and home. On the job, there was none of the slave-driving common on cotton plantations. They "worked under an extremely relaxed form of discipline — so much so that other whites objected to the breakdown of the traditional master—slave, black—white relationship, and the government intervened to impose such discipline as was considered necessary to perpetuate slavery as a system. In other words, other slave owners were not prepared to have tobacco manufacturers externalize costs by treating slaves so much better as to create problems in managing slaves elsewhere.

The whole pattern of slave relations in the antebellum tobacco industry was "hotly opposed by other whites in southern tobacco manufacturing towns". As a result "governmental authorities often deliberately interceded between manufacturing owners and slaves to maintain the black—white standards that these owners had allowed to slacken in the name of economic efficiency".[18]

Lumbering in the North Carolina swamps also required different work patterns and elicited different treatment from that of cotton field hands. Unlike other slave work, lumbering required a dispersion of workers through the swamps, with increased opportunities for escape — and therefore an increased necessity to reduce incentives to escape. Accordingly, contemporary observers noted that the slave lumberman "lives measurably as a free man", that no slave-driving "is attempted or needed", that they were paid in cash, and at least one had saved enough to operate as a money-lender to local whites! (He eventually bought his freedom with the proceeds.)[19] Slave divers in the Carolina swamps likewise were also dispersed and did underwater work requiring individual initiative and skill. They were "managed as freemen" and paid wages and bonuses, with the consequence that many insisted on working even when ill, in contrast to field slaves who took every opportunity to be absent from work.[20]

The point here is not that one incentive system was categorically more efficient than the other. Rather, it differed according to the work and according to the cost of knowledge to those who held the decision-making power.

One of the most common modifications of slavery in the antebellum South was the hiring out of urban slaves. About a third of the urban slaves worked as employees, typically living and working away from the slave owners, and paying some share of their earnings to him as the price of exemption from the harsh conditions of pure slavery. Some employers of urban slaves contracted directly with the slave owners, but many urban slaves chose their own employers and changed employers when they wanted to.

The degree of freedom among those urban slaves who were hired out was as bitterly resented by whites throughout the South as was that of slaves in the tobacco industry. There were likewise numerous government interventions to impose the kind of constraints deemed appropriate to a slave society. These government regulations were difficult to enforce in the case of urban slaves, since both the slaves and the slave owners had incentives to evade them. Urban slaves in general were dispersed among a wide variety of places and occupations, unlike slaves concentrated in a few tobacco factories which were easier to monitor.

Not all urban slaves — or even most — were hired out, but even those who were domestic servants in the city were less insulated than plantation slaves, and many circulated around the city on errands to the markets or elsewhere. Frederick

Douglass described the urban slave as "almost a free citizen".[21] He had been one himself. His escape illustrated one of the costs of urban slavery to slave owners. Urban slaves found it easier to acquire literacy, being away from the control of slave owners a significant part of the time, and usually having social contacts with urban "free persons of color" who often acquired literacy despite white efforts to prevent it. Accordingly, permanent escape was much more common among urban slaves than among plantation slaves. This in turn meant that slave owners were constrained in their treatment — especially punishment — of urban slaves, by the prospect of provoking an escape.

Among the signs of a relaxation of plantation slave discipline evident in an urban setting were informal social interactions with whites — including in drinking establishments and brothels — which undermind the rigid racial caste distinctions that perpetuated slavery at low cost. Bitter complaints about this from white citizens and authorities seemed less than fully effective, inasmuch as the same complaints continued for decades in southern cities, and often the same laws against it were passed again and again in the same communities, suggesting that previous laws had not had the anticipated effect. Knowledge cost differences made rigid control of a dispersed urban slave population much more difficult than similar repression of a slave population living under direct, round-the-clock white supervision on isolated farms and plantations.

It is significant that the proportion of mulatto children born to slave women was several times higher in the cities than on plantations. If these children were primarily a result of forcible rape, the opposite pattern would be expected — plantation slaves being far more constantly and repressively under the control of whites. What was peculiar about antebellum Southern cities was not only that racial caste distinctions were not as consistently maintained as on the plantation, but also that there was a chronic surplus of white men compared to white women, and a chronic surplus of black women compared to black men. Such demographic patterns, with any two groups, almost invariably lead to mixed childrn, whatever the economic or political system.

The Economics of Freedom

The same individual worker has different output potential as a slave and as a free worker. As a slave, his range of work possibilities is limited by the constraint that his escape possibilities be restricted. This involves not only a limitation of the tasks that can be performed by a person of a given capability, but also a limitation on the amount of capability that can be permitted to be developed in a person of a given potential. The same person can therefore be thought of as representing two possible streams of future output — one if under slavery, and another if free.

Economic theory predicts that, if an asset has different values in alternative uses, it will tend to be traded to the higher valued use. In a theoretically perfect economy, each slave would be more valuable as a free man, in purely economic terms, even aside from the value of freedom itself. Anyone may own the value of a given individual as a slave, but only that individual can own his value as a free man. Therefore, in an ideally functioning economy, each slave would be the highest bidder for himself. Each slave would purchase his freedom at a higher price than the slave owner could receive from any other bidder, and the whole system of slavery would be self-liquidating. That the slave has no money is no insurmountable problem, either in an ideal economy or in the real world, because capital markets exist which can finance all sorts of purchases with all sorts of risks and repayment plans. What is crucial is whether there are sufficient economic grounds for transferring the asset in the first place.

What does this theoretical construct have to do with the real world? It is important (1) in raising the question as to what really perpetuated slavery in the United States, and why, and (2) in explaining the transitory nature of bondage for many individuals and groups in many other societies in which serfdom, slavery, and other forms of bondage have existed.

In the ancient Greek and Roman world, it was well understood that the maximum economic gain to be made from an individual was by selling him his freedom. There were "many examples in the manumission records from

Delphi after 200 BC" of slave purchase of their freedom.[22] Both pirates and governments preferred to ransom foreign captives rather than retain them as slaves,[23] or sell them in the slave market. Self-purchase and ransom prices were higher than slave market prices in the ancient Mediterranean world.[24] Moreover, the economic advantages of modifying slavery were also recognized. In ancient times, as in the antebellum South, there were hired slaves "who lived apart from the owner's residence, working at occupations of any sort and paying to their owners all or some percentage of their earnings".[25] In societies where a wide variety of occupations were filled by slaves, there was "generally mild treatment" and no serious slave uprisings.[26] Many ancient societies had substantial numbers of former slaves, even though slavery itself had not been abolished. Manumission procedures were legally available and socially accepted. Even in some modern western hemisphere countries in the nineteenth century, more people were freed while slavery continued as an institution than were freed by the abolition of slavery.[27]

The institutional and legal problems of arranging loans for slaves to purchase themselves meant that there were not zero transaction costs, and therefore no instant self-destruction of slavery, as with ideal capital markets. However, what is remarkable is how many different financial processes have existed for slave self-purchase down through the centuries. Ancient Rome legally recognized the slave's property or *peculium*, which could be applied toward purchasing freedom, and any bargain with the slave owner was enforced by the government.[28] Lending institutions in ancient Greece — among other places — enabled the slave to purchase his freedom with a loan, repayable in installments.[29] In nineteenth-century Latin America, Catholic priests served as independent intermediaries guaranteeing the fulfillment of contract terms for freedom between master and slave.[30]

In short, the creation of capital market institutions to effect slave self-purchase was not an insurmountable obstacle. Why, then, did it not happen in the antebellum South, after having been widespread in slave societies of ancient times, or even in some contemporary Latin slave societies?

Southern state governments intervened to severely restrict or virtually prohibit slaves and slave owners from making such mutually beneficial transactions. In some states, it took a specific act of the state legislature for each slave to become free, and this was granted only under extraordinary circumstances, such as some act of heroism by a slave, saving lives in the white community.

Initially, in colonial America, manumission of slaves had been relatively easy, and the Quakers freed their slaves *en masse* after deciding that slavery was morally wrong. In the ideological climate of immediate post-Revolutionary America, many individuals in the north freed their slaves, and northern states began to outlaw slavery. It was in the South that legal barriers to manumission grew ever more restrictive and ultimately prohibitory.

How did the South differ from the north, and from those ancient slave societies in which masses of individuals regularly made the transition from slaves to free men, even while slavery itself continued as an institution? As already noted, pure slavery is most economically efficient with routine tasks, such as the production of cotton, and by virtue of its soil and climate the South became the center of slavery, and the South's best cotton growing regions — as in the Mississippi delta — had more slaves than free citizens. By contrast slaves in the northern states were a very small proportion of the population, as they were in Homeric Greece.[31]

The demographic composition of the South put the manumission of slaves in an entirely different light. A substantial percentage of the total population of the South consisted of a racially distinct group of slaves. The freeing of slaves under these circumstances entailed external costs on the white citizenry as a whole, including (1) increased costs of holding and controlling the remaining slaves, and (2) political costs from the presence of freedmen emerging from a slavery in which they had been kept ignorant and demoralized. The South was not in the position of ancient Greece, where slavery was an incidental feature of the society, but more like that of the Roman Republic in the first century BC, when the slave population "attained proportions never before known" and where slave revolts "occurred intermittently".[32] The South need not look back to the revolt of Spartacus for examples of the dangers of slave uprisings. A blood uprising in Santo Domingo in 1793 spread panic through the South, as did a smaller uprising of American slaves under Nat Turner in 1831, followed by increased repression of free blacks and even of whites whose ideological conformity on the issue of slavery was suspect.[33]

In economic terms, southern state governments acted as if they realized the external costs entailed by a free black population, and especially literate free blacks, and so intervened to prevent market transactions between slaves and slave owners that would have produced a larger population of "free persons of color". Visible racial differences between slaves and slave owners was a peculiarity of modern slavery, not characteristic of ancient slavery, where slaves included both captives in war and members of the same society reduced to bondage for debt or other reasons. Ancient slavery therefore produced no such group solidarity among either slaves or free citizens as to create large external costs of manumission. The presence of masses of freedmen in ancient societies did not imperil the continued existence of slavery, nor did any visible stigma attach to them or their offspring as a result of their former condition of servitude. The Roman Emperor Diocletian was the son of slaves who had been freed.

THE "PROFITABILITY" OF SLAVERY

One of the oldest controversies among economists and historians revolves around the question of whether slavery was economically profitable.[34] More than 200 years ago, Adam Smith declared slavery unprofitable, due to its lack of adequate incentives. Thus, although the wealth consumed by a slave might be less than that of a free worker, his output was considered so much less that the labor cost per unit of output would be higher under slavery than freedom. Although work done by slaves appears to be cheap, according to Smith, it is "in the end the dearest of any". Smith explained the persistence of slavery by the slave owner's pride, which "makes him love to domineer".[35] Smith also rejected the racial inferiority justification for slavery, suggesting instead that the Africans enslaved in America were probably superior to the slave owners.[36]

Smith's total rejection of slavery — both morally and economically — set a pattern followed by classical economists such as Ricardo, J. S. Mill, and J. E. Cairnes, who elaborated these themes in his book *The Slave Power* in 1862.[37] These views were challenged by some southern historians,[38] and much later — in the twentieth century — by economists using econometric techniques.[39] Their data and analysis led them to conclude that, by one means or another — but especially by working slaves longer hours and more years than free workers — slavery achieved more output than other economic systems under comparable circumstances.

In the course of these numerous, sporadic, eruptions of controversy over the economic efficiency of slavery, the questions have changed, along with the answers. At one extreme, the question is whether the individual slave owner actually profitted by investing in slaves as compared to alternative investment opportunities available, or whether slave owners persisted — and, indeed, bid up slave prices over time — for "irrational" reasons of one sort or another. At the other extreme is the question whether slavery was, on net balance, beneficial to people as a whole — including slaves as well as slave owners. The fact that force had to be used to capture, control, and restrain slaves is evidence to the contrary.

Another important question is whether slavery produced net benefits to the non-slave population of the society as a whole. Slavery could well have been profitable to slave owners, and yet create so many external costs as to make its economic impact negative on the white population as a whole. We have already noted some of those costs — loss of freedom and diversity of views, repelling many people with skills and resources valuable to the region — but more generally, it is apparent empirically that the incomes of the white population of the United States has been lowest in that region in which slavery has existed. Within the South, those parts in which slavery was particularly concentrated (Mississippi, Alabama, and other deep South states) have long had the very lowest incomes among white Southerners. This does not prove cause and effect, but it does present a challenge to find an alternative explanation for this striking geographic pattern of white income variation, and it does undermine the belief that non-slave-owning whites benefitted economically from slavery.

One of the bases of claims for "compensation" or "reparations" to contemporary blacks for the enslavement of their ancestors is that whites in general profited, even if they were not slave owners and even if their ancestors arrived after slavery was abolished, but still shared in economic benefits made possible by slavery. If slavery produced no net profits to whites as a whole (deducting the Civil War and other external costs), then "compensation" claims would have to use some other rationale.

"Compensation" based on pain and suffering would apply to the slaves themselves, who are long dead. Compensation to their descendants for disadvantages the latter suffer as the descendants of slaves would have to define some baseline from which to measure their losses. Is that baseline where these descendants would be if their ancestors had never been enslaved? But if that baseline is the difference between the average standard of living in Africa compared to the average standard of living of black Americans, the grotesque conclusion of this arithmetic might be that blacks pay whites compensation. If the baseline is premised on the assumption that blacks would have voluntarily immigrated to the United States, and would have earned the "national average" income in the absence of slavery and discrimination, then it makes two highly unlikely assumptions, given that there has been very little emigration from Africa, and the wide diversity among American ethnic groups precludes any assumptions that any group — especially from a non-urban, non-industrial, background — would earn the national average income.

SUMMARY AND IMPLICATIONS

Slavery as an economic system is an extreme example of a decision-making process in which the power is concentrated in one group of people while the knowledge of individual capabilities is concentrated in another. This central fact determined the kinds of work that could be performed under pure slavery, such as cotton growing and other tasks in which monitoring costs are sufficiently low as to mitigate the effects of the separation of knowledge and power. That central knowledge cost problem also explains the modifications of slavery when tasks required slave performances of a kind not easily monitored — more skilled, judgmental, or isolated work.

Substantial external costs were entailed by slavery in the special form in which it existed in the antebellum South, with slaves and slave owners being of visibly different ancestry. Racial sympathies or solidarity between former slaves and current slaves raised the security costs of slavery, engendered repression of "free persons of color", and promoted laws severely restricting the manumission of slaves. Unlike other systems of bondage in which the slave or serf might purchase freedom, the government prohibitions on such transactions meant that slavery could only be ended by other government power — in this case, by the Civil War.

If the doctrine that the white population as a whole derived economic benefits from the enslavement of blacks is treated as a testable hypothesis, much evidence suggests the opposite — the location of slave concentrations being also locations of white incomes below the national average, both during and after slavery. Among the white ethnic groups above the national average in income, most arrived after the Civil War. The highest income ethnic group — the Jews — arrived overwhelmingly after the Civil War, and even those Jews who lived in the antebellum South seldom owned slaves.

CHAPTER SIX

Government and Minorities

Government has three roles in the economy that bear on the economic fate of ethnic groups: (1) government provides a legal framework within which transactors can make their own economic (and other) decisions; (2) government can reduce the options available to the transactors; and (3) government can redistribute the fruits of economic transactions.

Government is inextricably bound up with politics, even in non-democratic nations. Therefore, the role of government is greatly influenced by the incentives and constraints facing those individuals who pursue politics as a career. This simple fact is often overlooked in policy discussions in which the government is treated as if it were an external agency correcting the deficiencies of other institutions — more or less "the public interest" personified. While public spirit and self-sacrifice have characterized some statesmen, to expect this to be the sole or dominant incentive among political decision-makers as a whole is to ignore thousands of years of human history.

GOVERNMENT AS FRAMEWORK

The diffusion of knowledge and the concentration of power can be reconciled by having economic decisions made by individual transactors, and the terms agreed upon enforced by the government. In addition to these explicitly contractual agreements, there are virtually universally shared desires — such as security of person and belongings — which can be treated as implicit contracts to be enforced by the government. Depending upon the specific nature of the government, the population (or segments thereof) may have more or less "rights" — meaning, empirically, options for which government force is available to the individual.

The stable framework of behavioral expectations provided by government enables individuals to interact with less fear of physical or economic harm from one another, fewer and less costly precautions, and more willingness to undertake joint actions whose benefits accrue in the future. Much of this beneficial effect comes from the stability of the framework rather than the intrinsic merits of its specific provisions. For example, driving on the right-hand side of the road may be no more advantageous than driving on the left-hand side of the road, but either system may be far preferable to *ad hoc* decisions by each driver.

In the case of low-income ethnic groups attempting to rise, the degree of stability of the governmental framework is especially important. Typically, low-income ethnic groups are relative newcomers — either to the country or (in the case of blacks or American Indians) to the urban economy and society. It is difficult enough to adjust to a new situation, but adjusting to a situation that is itself continually changing is obviously even more of a problem. To what extent has the government maintained stable "rules of the game", within which ethnic minorities could adjust? A brief historical sketch of blacks may suggest some of the problems.

Initially, Africans brought to the United States in the early seventeenth century became indentured servants, like most white immigrants, and were freed at the end of a few years. Somewhere around the middle of the seventeenth century, this was changed to perpetual slavery. Free blacks in the early seventeenth century had essentially the same rights as their white contemporaries, but these rights came to be taken away, one by one, with the development of slavery and its attendant efforts to control and humble the entire black population. The post-Revolutionary War era led to abolition of slavery in the north, and a relaxation of restrictions on "free persons of color". But within a generation, new government restrictions began to be imposed on the occupations, mobility, legal status, etc., of free Negroes. Moreover, the enforcement of these state laws was highly varied with respect to both time and place. Free blacks were voting, even in some Southern states, in the 1820s but, by the mid-nineteenth century, all Southern and even many northern states were barring blacks from voting — but in less than a generation these laws were repealed. In the South, Reconstruction saw blacks holding political office on a large scale, from local officials to the Congress of the United States. Just one generation later, Jim Crow laws and extra-legal terrorism against black voters almost totally eliminated black officials from Southern political life. In the national government, the slow progress of black employees over the decades was suddenly reversed by the Woodrow Wilson administration, which introduced segregation among federal employees and began a drastic cutback of blacks in non-menial jobs. In the war of 1812 Commodore Perry's crew had been one-fourth black, but by the 1920s there was literally not one black sailor in the navy. In the 1930s, the New Deal began a slow reversal again, toward better treatment of blacks — a pattern now a little more than a generation old.

In broad historical terms, government has changed the rules of the game for blacks in virtually every generation. These have been fundamental changes stretching across the spectrum from education to housing to jobs to voting. Nor have blacks been unique. The changing interpretations and violations of Indian treaties are an historical scandal. With respect to European immigrants, the largest and most open migration in human history was suddenly brought to a screeching halt in the 1920s. Japanese Americans, who were initially welcomed as workers in California in the nineteenth century, were later segregated in the schools, barred from numerous occupations, forbidden to own land, locked up *en masse* during World War II — and then, in less than a decade, all these trends reversed. Residential segregation of Orientals collapsed, high rates of intermarriage with whites followed, along with national political office holding — and then even preferential treatment as "disadvantaged" minorities, while earning above-average incomes.

The point here is not so much the individual merits or demerits of these various policies considered in isolation. The point is the sheer *volatility* of government policy toward ethnic groups. Nor is the United States unique in this. Similar patterns have occurred in other multi-ethnic societies. Political authorities in many countries have often turned against ethnic minorities once allowed to prosper in peace. The brutal mass expulsions of East Indians under the Amin regime in Uganda, the slaughter of the Ibos in Nigeria, and the severe current official discrimination against the Chinese in Indonesia are recent examples of a pattern of volatile government policy changes toward minorities that goes back for centuries. Historically, Germany was one of the most open, tolerant, and favorable countries in the world for Jews — until the generation of Hitler and the Holocaust. American Jews were so favorably disposed toward Germany as of World War I that the US government cracked down on Jewish newspapers in the United States on grounds of undermining the war effort.[1] From World War I to World War II was less than a quarter of a century.

In view of the historic unpredictability of government policy toward ethnic minorities, it is perhaps unsurprising that some of the most dramatic rises from poverty to affluence in the United States have been among groups who did *not* attempt to use the political route to economic advancement — notably the Chinese, the Japanese, and the Jews. Chinese American leaders long ago made a deliberate decision to keep out of the political arena, while concentrating on economic progress.[2] Conversely, the group with the longest and most intimate involvement with the US government — American Indians, especially on reservations — have long been at the bottom of the economic ladder by such indices as family income or unemployment rates, not to mention restrictions on the use of their own property and other paternalistic policies of the Bureau of Indian Affairs. The most politically successful American ethnic group — the Irish — was also the slowest rising of the nineteenth-century

European immigrant groups.

Nevertheless, it is taken as axiomatic in many quarters that political action is the key to economic advance. Even writers who use the recent economic advancement of blacks through government policy as proof of the power of group political action nevertheless note — as an isolated curiosity — that northern blacks have had *declining* voter registration and voter turnout since 1940.[3] Southern blacks of course vote much more often than before — but this is a consequence rather than a cause of federal government policy.

At particular historic junctures, governmental policy may be beneficial to particular ethnic groups. It is the long-run reliance on political action that is questionable in view of the unpredictability of political trends in general. It has been said that in politics "overnight is a lifetime". Even in governmental institutions less subject to electoral shifts — the Supreme Court, for example — profound changes can take place in a span that is relatively short in historical perspective. Throughout much of the nineteenth century, advocates of the cause of blacks looked upon the Supreme Court as a bitter enemy rather than a protector of rights — and decisions from *Dred Scott*[4] in 1857 to *Plessy* v. *Ferguson*[5] in 1896 gave ample support to this view. However, in the twentieth century, the Supreme Court has become the primary hope of civil rights advocates. In an even shorter time frame, restrictive covenants were upheld by the Supreme Court in 1926 and declared unconstitutional just 22 years later. The same attorney who attacked restrictive covenants before the Supreme Court in 1926 defended school segregation before that Court in 1954. In short, the supposedly stable legal and constitutional framework is also subject to drastic changes, which are still more common in electoral politics.

All this has a bearing on a subsidiary theme of some, that there is an establishment relentlessly pursuing its aims behind the political scene. There are special interest groups of whom this is true, and politicians who engage in corruption and cover-up. What has been lacking — certainly as regards ethnic groups — is any stable, long-run policy, whether benign or sinister.

GOVERNMENT REDUCTION OF OPTIONS

Economic analysis would lead us to expect that people would more fully satisfy their own respective preferences with a larger set of options, where the larger set includes all the items in a smaller set. Yet there are many government laws, regulations, and policies whose effect is simply to reduce existing options without adding any new ones. Minimum wage laws, rent control, and interest rate ceilings, for example, simply outlaw certain ranges of transactions terms. Housing codes, occupational licensing laws, or Jim Crow laws have made certain kinds of transactions illegal, regardless of their terms. None of these laws and policies add any options. They simply remove some existing options.

Housing Quality
In housing, such government programs as "slum clearance" or urban renewal have been justified by studies showing former slum dwellers living in "better" housing. But this is no new option. Slum dwellers always had the option of moving into better housing, at the sacrifice of some non-housing goods they were purchasing. All that "slum clearance" has done is force them to make a trade-off they did not want to make — i.e. to become worse off by their own preference standards.

In special circumstances, the negative effects of some transactions on non-transacting parties may justify option-reduction applied to transactors — precisely in order that the excluded preferences of non-transactors be taken into account. Air and water pollution are classic examples of these external effects. In such cases, there is no net reduction of options of all the affected parties, even though the options of the immediate transactors may be reduced. Housing has sometimes been alleged to be another case of external effects, as in the proposition that "slums breed crime".

That criminality and slums have gone together down through history is demonstrable, but the direction of causation is by no means clear. The same attitudes that create crime may also create slums. It is not a question of which theory sounds more plausible *a priori* but (1) what different consequences follow from the two different theories, and (2) which set of consequences is found in factual data. To make such an empirical test possible, "slums" must be defined independently of the amount of crime taking place in neighborhoods with structures of given physical characteristics. It is possible to make crime-breeding slums a circular conclusion by simply defining physically run-down buildings or neighborhoods without high crime rates as not "really" slums. The great problem with circular statements is that what they are explicitly saying — which is nothing — is irrefutable, while what they are insinuating may be fraught with meaning and completely wrong.

As the proportion of physically substandard housing units declined in the 1960s, the crime rates soared. New York's Chinatown was once one of the lowest crime rate sections of the city, despite older and more run-down buildings than in Harlem. The later crime increase in New York's Chinatown — and Chinatowns in other cities — was not associated with housing deterioration but with the arrival of new Chinese immigrants from a different culture in Hong Kong.

The central role of people and their values — rather than physical surroundings — raises the question of whether much of the physical deterioration is not itself a result of the same set of values, or lack of values. Brand new government housing projects around the country have become instant slums as former slum dwellers moved in. All the characteristics of old-fashioned slums — filth, noise, violence, and physical destruction of property — have reappeared in government housing projects. Even such a zealous nineteenth-century reformer as Jacob Riis, who called slums "nurseries of crime",[6] also noted that some people "carry their slums with them wherever they go".[7]

Labor

In labor markets as well as in housing markets, government reduces options in general — and the options of low-income ethnic groups in particular. In nineteenth-century American cities the lowest jobs, as well as the worst slum housing, belonged almost exclusively to the various immigrant groups from Europe. On the West Coast, such jobs and such housing was also the fate of immigrants from China, and in the South it was the fate of newly freed blacks.

Government regulation of labor markets has included occupational licensing laws, minimum wage laws, regulation of working conditions, and child labor laws. We have also seen (chapters 2 and 3) how minimum wage laws reduce the price of discrimination, thereby increasing the quantity. Such laws also harm low-income ethnic groups in their role as less skilled or less productive workers for whatever reason (inexperience, cultural patterns at variance with industrial requirements of punctuality, discipline, cooperation, etc.). Restrictive occupational licensing laws also reduce the employer's cost of discrimination by creating a surplus of job applicants. In addition, occupational licensing standards may themselves be discriminatory. For example, during the 1930s, when many skilled Jewish refugees were entering the United States, "a US citizenship requirement was added to most occupational licensure laws".[8] In the South, around the turn of the century, licensing examinations for black plumbers were conducted by white examiners, who almost invariably "failed" them, even though the same individual blacks "have easily met the requirements elsewhere".[9] With the rise of government-supported labor unions having complete dominance over particular occupations — notably in the railroads and the construction trades — union membership was tantamount to occupational licensing, and was used to keep out (or drive out) blacks.

In both the craft union situation and in explicit occupational licensing, it was the turning over of governmental powers to private interests that was the key to the effectiveness of the exclusion. Occupational licensing boards are almost invariably in the hands of existing practitioners. With the Wagner Act in 1935, the government made employer recognition of existing employees' unions mandatory, and therefore put into the hands of incumbent workers the power to exclude other workers.

Government control of working conditions would seem to be racially or ethnically neutral, but historically its impact has been quite different for different groups, regardless of whether or not this was the intent. In the nineteenth century, the prime target of government regulation of working conditions was the "sweatshop" where long hours in run-down buildings was the rule. These sweatshop workers were almost entirely immigrants, and the classic examples were the sweatshops among the Jewish workers on the lower east side of New York. Again, the government did nothing directly to create better conditions — that would have cost vast sums of money — but instead simply outlawed some existing conditions, or reduced the options open to the transactors. One of the other options was to have the work performed in the home, where it was more difficult for government inspectors to monitor hours or working conditions.

A contemporary account of a typical nineteenth-century east side tenement mentioned, along with "smells of cabbage, onions, or frying fish" on every floor, also "whirring sewing machines behind closed doors, betraying what goes on within . . ."[10] The men, women, and children — mostly Jewish in this era — worked long hours in their homes. But, although reformers and historians have spoken of this as "exploitation", they also acknowledged that (1) the sweatshop owners themselves made little money, despite long hours of work,[11] and (2) among the Jewish workers on New York's lower east side, the long hours were hardly necessary to keep body and soul together, despite their low pay, "more than half of which goes into the bank".[12] In short, despite the sinister innuendos and indignant language which have become standard in describing this situation, the actual evidence suggests nothing more than employers and employees making the most of such limited options as they had, given the technology, skill, and wealth at their disposal. Government added to none of these three requisites, but only reduced their ability to optimize according to their own knowledge and preferences. In view of the later economic progress of Jews, it is by no means clear that their understanding of their situation was not at least as good as that of the reformers, who tried vainly to stop them from doing what they felt they had to do.

Nor is it obvious that the greater success of twentieth-century reformers in forcing contemporary low-income minority youths out of the labor force has been a blessing, especially given the evidence of a correlation between youth unemployment and crime.[13] These reform efforts have included not only control of working conditions, but also compulsory school attendance laws which make full-time work illegal for those of school age. Here, at least, the claim can be made that the government adds to the available options by providing schooling free of charge to the users. However, the forced retention of teenagers who do not want to be in school is hardly costless to the other students, or to the process of education. A study of changes in the compulsory attendance law in Britain showed that the oldest group retained in school had the highest delinquency rate, both before and after that age was raised — thirteen-year-olds before, and fourteen-year-olds after.[14] It was apparently not the fact of being age thirteen or fourteen that was crucial — it was the length of time being forcibly retained past the point where the process had become counterproductive for both the student and the school.

It is often taken as axiomatic that more years in school is "a good thing" — virtually without limit, in defiance of the economic logic of diminishing returns and of inherent trade-offs between one good and another. But, once the idea of trade-off is accepted, it is easy to understand that the terms of trade-off may differ from individual to individual and from group to group, implying that different amounts of schooling may be optimal in different circumstances. Moreover, those closest to the situation — the parents and children — may have more knowledge of their options than distant social theorists. But when the decision as to length of schooling is made by third-party observers and enforced by government, it is more likely to reflect some crude compromise between what the poor prefer and what the middle class prefer — very much like "decent housing".

Insofar as such reform efforts are spearheaded by the educated, and by educators — and seconded by labor unions, with a vested interest in restricting the labor supply — the tendency of compulsory attendance laws is to keep youths in school well past the point where they and their parents would have preferred that they be working. Evidence for this hypothesis includes both high rates of truancy and in-school delinquency in low-income ethnic neighborhoods — much more than in past periods, when the school-leaving age was lower.

Transactions Terms

More direct government intervention, with the explicit intention of affecting ethnic minorities, has been evident in such laws and policies as Jim Crow laws in the South, and "equal opportunity" laws and "affirmative action" policies more recently at the federal level.

Deliberately discriminatory laws have been part of the history of the United States, and many other countries. If such laws were always effective, Jews and Chinese would be poverty-stricken around the world, instead of generally prosperous. Even in the antebellum South, where severely restrictive laws kept the "free persons of color" out of many occupations, the economic advancement of this group continued on up to the Civil War, and their descendants continued to prosper and provide a disproportionate amount of twentieth-century black leadership. [15] The problems facing a government seeking to enforce discrimination as a social policy are very similar to those facing governments seeking the social betterment of some groups: (1) insufficiency of knowledge, (2) monitoring costs, and (3) individual transactors' incentives to behave at variance with the government policy.

Discrimination, like any other government policy, requires a certain amount of knowledge of current conditions and of future trends to be effective. When Jews were kept out of many occupations central to the landed economy of feudalism, they were forced into commercial and industrial occupations peripheral to feudalism but central to later emerging capitalism, giving the Jews an historic advantage — obviously contrary to the purposes of the policy. Even where government has a generally accurate assessment of conditions and trends, it faces the problem of monitoring numerous transactors who have incentives to behave differently from the way government wants them to behave. The difficulties of enforcing conditions deemed appropriate to urban slaves in the antebellum South indicates something of the magnitude of the monitoring problem, even when those being monitored are easily distinguished from the general population by skin color.

The historic poverty of postbellum Southern blacks may seem to suggest the effectiveness of the discriminatory policies of Southern states. However, given the enormous racial difference in initial wealth and — perhaps even more important — in human capital immediately after the Civil War, even with an ideally non-discriminating government, it would have taken unprecedented achievements for blacks to have closed the gap in a few generations — especially since white income was growing all the while.[16] As it was, with governments that were very far from ideal, black income grew at a higher rate than white income after the Civil War.[17] In short, black—white income gaps are hardly an accurate measure of the effectiveness of discriminatory government policy. Conversely, the highly controversial "affirmative action" government policies in recent years have produced little over-all pay or employment changes for blacks relative to whites, as measured empirically by a number of economists.[18] The point here is not to claim that all government discrimination has been totally ineffective. Economic questions are generally incremental rather than categorical.

Why have government policies — whether discriminatory or preferential — had less impact than anticipated? The uniform transactions terms (including no transactions in some high-level positions) preferred by a discriminatory government are almost certain to differ from the variety of transactions terms preferred by individuals in differing circumstances and having preferences differing from one another as well as from the government. Moreover, economic competition especially rewards those who find cheaper ways to produce, or ways to make more sales — including producing with proscribed workers and selling to proscribed customers (racial "block-busting" in real estate, for example). Those potential transactors facing the greatest barriers tend to offer the most favorable terms, by agreeing to work for lower wages or to pay higher rents.

Monitoring millions of individual transactors who have

incentives to circumvent government policy is a formidable task in any context, including Prohibition. Even in South Africa, policies to exclude black workers from various higher positions have been eroded despite restrictive laws against Africans and government quotas for Europeans. To effectively maintain apartheid in the economy, the government has had to resort to laws which appear on the surface to be non-racial — minimum wage laws and equal pay laws — but which serve the key purpose of reducing monitoring costs, by eliminating the incentive to evade the discrimination policies. It is relatively easy to monitor observance of wage minima and equal pay for equal work and, insofar as this is done, it is far less necessary to monitor hiring practices, for the incentive to hire native Africans is eliminated, once their pay has been raised to parity with Europeans.

"Equal opportunity" laws and policies — hiring "without regard" to race, color, or nationality — represent less interference with ordinary economic incentives than either discriminatory or preferential policies. It is, therefore, perhaps not surprising that they seem more effective. Black income as a percentage of white income rose significantly after passage of the Civil Rights Act of 1964 — whether because of that Act or because the changed public opinion which made the Act possible also made possible a reduction in hiring discrimination. There were many independent contemporary indications of changed public opinion on race and ethnicity.

Housing Distribution
In consumer markets, the effect of political versus market decision-making can be seen in the very different history of housing for Jews in Europe and blacks in the United States. Historically, the term "ghetto" originated in medieval Europe, where Jews lived in sections of town designated by political authorities, and surrounded by walls and gates that were locked at night. Black neighborhoods today are called ghettos only metaphorically, by extension. As the Jewish population grew, the ghetto simply became more crowded, except for political decisions permitting expansion at

infrequent and unpredictable intervals. By contrast, every northern urban ghetto in the United States has developed out of neighborhoods that were white at the turn of the century. Harlem, the oldest and most famous of the northern black urban communities was still predominantly white as late as 1910.[19] Black ghettos expanded much more steadily and rapidly through market transactions in the United States than did Jewish ghettos through political processes in Europe.

These empirical results are at variance with frequently reiterated assertions that government action in general, and court action in particular, are essential if blacks are to obtain desegregated housing. To have housing decisions made through the market, rather than through the political process, means "abandoning the Negro to the slum-ghetto that 'private enterprise' has made ready for him",[20] according to this viewpoint. This conclusion was treated as axiomatic, so there was no need to examine evidence comparing the consequences of political versus economic modes of decision-making. Once it was decided that the economic results were displeasing, the next step was the familiar *non sequitur* that political results would be better.

In practice, however, as we have noted in chapter 4, the era of the greatest residential integration in American cities was the last quarter of the nineteenth century — at a time when racially restrictive covenants were legal, when courts took little interest in the rights of blacks, and when black political power was negligible (especially in the northern cities that were residentially integrated). Conversely, although the Supreme Court's striking down of racially restrictive covenants in 1948 was hailed as a landmark in the struggle for integrated housing, in cold fact it made very little difference in the amount of residential segregation.

Historically, government has itself been a major promoter of residential segregation. A number of municipal governments made residential segregation official policy early in the twentieth century,[21] and the Federal Housing Administration *required* racial segregation as a precondition for federally insured loans on into the late 1940s.[22] The current swing of the political pendulum is in the direction of residentially mixing not only races but social classes.

However, insofar as this takes the form of simply reducing options, it may be relatively ineffective. For example, a judge ordered that 75 per cent of the public housing built in Chicago be so located as to place black tenants in white neighborhoods — but the only net result was to halt public housing construction in Chicago.[23] Nor is the issue necessarily racial. Black middle-class residents have bitterly fought the building of low-income housing projects near them,[24] and there is a great difference in the general public's reactions to housing for the elderly from their reactions to housing for low-income families of any race or ethnicity:

> Subsidized elderly housing, which does not carry the threat of crime, vandalism, or deterioration of local schools, can be built almost anywhere without much protest, but any sizable project for poor families has always been extremely hard to plant in a neighborhood where people are paying their own way.[25]

In short, the *behavior pattern* of a group is the crucial variable in both racial and non-racial contexts. It was the crucial variable in the residential racial integration of northern cities in the late nineteenth century, in the severe segregation that succeeded it after the massive migration of southern blacks, and in the *internal* segregation of different classes of blacks, Jews, Mexicans, etc., from other members of their own respective groups. Individuals whose behavior patterns differ most from that of their own racial or ethnic group suffer most from group sorting and labelling, and it is precisely such individuals who have spearheaded the drive for housing "integration"[26] — meaning, in fact, class segregation. Racial segregation inhibited class segregation by lumping all blacks together. Once government policy begins to mean random redistribution of people, black middle-class "integrationists" oppose it.

There has never been random distribution of people, whether in housing, jobs, or other activities. Jewish immigrants from different countries or at different stages of acculturation and socio-economic mobility likewise separated residentially. There was a "separateness and discontinuity" of these local Jewish areas from one another,[27] and sometimes a repeated migration of individuals from one

to the other in response to their own acculturation or to the
inflow of less acculturated newcomers: "he becomes irritated
by the presence of his fellow-Jews, more Jewish than
himself"[28] — all this to the accompaniment of mutual
recriminations.[29]

Among Italian immigrants, residential clustering occurred
according to the province, city, or even village of origin in
Italy.[30] This reflected the highly localized loyalties of
southern Italy,[31] from which most Italian Americans
originated. They only begin to think of themselves as Italian
after reaching America.[32]

Among the present-day descendants of southern European
immigrants, half would have to be relocated, if a random
distribution of people were to be achieved.[33] This much
residential "segregation" from the larger society persists half a
century after mass immigration from that part of the world
ended. The very phrase "segregation" is ambiguous —
lumping together both *ex ante* restrictions and *ex post* results.
One reason why even a successful "open housing" campaign
changes residential clustering patterns very little is that many
people prefer being clustered, even when they are not
segregated by the larger society.

Neither the market nor the government has "solved" the
"problem" of residential clustering. The very conception of a
problem with a solution may be fallacious here, as in many
other areas of decision-making. There are highly disparate
values within and between groups, and one way of coping
with these differences is separation — spatial or psychic. It
has long been noted that there is usually less spatial
separation between blacks and whites in the South because
there are such well developed psychic mechanisms of
separation there. Studies have shown that even those blacks
or Jews who express belief in integration prefer living where
half the people are members of their own group.[34] But such a
result is incompatible with the preferences of other groups.
There is no reason to expect that there exists anything that
can be called a "solution" in such circumstances. There may
be something that meets the standard of Pareto optimality —
a situation in which each individual is as well off as he can be,
by his own standards, without making others worse off by

their standards. There is no reason to expect a government-imposed reduction of options to move the situation in that direction.

In addition to housing segregation, government policies affect low-income ethnic groups in other ways. Both historically and at present, low-income ethnic groups have arrived in the cities after others have had first choice of locations, and have typically occupied the most desirable ones. In addition to occupying larger individual quantities of the most desirable urban land, the more affluent classes typically also make recreational use of vast amounts of land in the countryside, in such activities as camping, hunting, boating, and skiing. While the residential land is typically allocated through economic processes, recreational land is more likely to be allocated through political processes — as state and national parks and forests, or land "protected" by laws on coastal preservation or zoning. The land owned and kept out of the market by state or national government is far from negligible. In California, for example, more than half the land in the state is government-owned, and in Alaska more than 90 per cent of the land is owned by the federal government.

While the affluent, by definition, have individually larger amounts of money than the non-affluent, the sheer numbers of the latter put far more total financial resources at their disposal. Economic transactors who are seeking to maximize their total profit would much rather make ten million dollars from 10,000 people who are not rich than to make one million dollars from one millionaire. The net result is that ethnic groups newly arriving in the city bid great quantities of land and housing away from the affluent, either directly or through realtors, banks, landlords, or other intermediaries. The arrival of Irish and German immigrants in New York in the 1840s brought a transfer of property in the central city from the affluent natives to the impoverished newcomers, and an expansion of the city as a whole, with the affluent leading the exodus.[35] The same scenario was to be followed again and again, in innumerable urban centers, for more than a century, with blacks, Hispanics, Orientals, and others taking on the role of urban newcomers in later times.

No such pattern has been evident in the vast recreational land area under political control, despite the widespread assumption that the poor are at an advantage in the political process and at a disadvantage in the economic process. But in the economic process it is the *total* financial resources that count, while in the political process it is often the *average* level of understanding of the issues that is critical. If an issue is very clearly understood by all, the numerous poor have a political advantage over the few rich. But many political issues are quite complex — or lend themselves to being made complicated by rhetoric and obfuscation — and in these cases the poor, the less educated, the newly arrived, can be at a decisive disadvantage in the political process.

In the case of recreational land use, the issue is not even posed in terms of alternative sets of people competing for given land. Instead, the affluent who make up such groups as the Sierra Club pose the issue as one of disembodied principles about "the environment", "ecology", "congestion", or preventing the "misuse" or "spoiling" of "nature". That these goals have some positive value is neither unusual nor decisive; it is typical of economic competition that different sets of values are weighed against each other. Clearly, if half the land in a state is kept off the market by the government, the price of the other half is going to be far higher than otherwise, and this means far higher prices for buying houses or renting apartments throughout the state. Where the land along the coast is either government-owned or kept from being used for small homes or apartments by coastal commissions or zoning boards, this means that other people stay bottled up in the inner city away from fresh air. Insofar as the affluent succeed politically in blocking the construction of power plants, this raises electricity rates. Insofar as they block construction of highways or motels near the wilderness areas, they keep access to such areas limited to those with the time, money, and leisure to hike in or to maintain clubs or other private facilities in the area. In short, the policies of affluent recreational interests ("environmentalists") do involve a trade-off between the well-being of different sets of people, even though phrased in highly abstract principles about "nature", "ecology", etc. Although this has been going on for generations, it is only quite recently that any question has been raised about such things from the standpoint of low-income ethnic groups. Differences in the average level of understanding and promotion of self-interest (suitably packaged as the general well-being) often put low-income ethnic groups at more of a disadvantage in the political arena than in the economic arena.

In economic transactions, it usually matters little how much the individual transactor understands about the underlying process involved. He needs only know his own preferences and alternatives. The extreme example would be the immediate postbellum blacks in the South, who were illiterate, unable to count, and largely unprotected by the law — and who still were able to get improved housing and higher pay through ordinary market transactions. The underlying processes behind transaction terms need not be understood by both sides, so long as those transactors who do understand have to compete with each other. But the low-income labor market and the low-income housing market are too vast for transactors to be anything other than competitors.

GOVERNMENT REDISTRIBUTION

The redistribution of income by government is one area in which political activity seems most promising for low-income minorities. However, even here the picture is not nearly as clear-cut as it might appear for a number of reasons:

1 The great variety of progressive and regressive government transfers makes their net effects uncertain.

2 All that is taken from the taxpayers for the benefit of the poor does not in fact go to the poor.

3 Transfers are not simply added to the earnings the recipient would have otherwise; remaining below some officially defined level of income is a precondition for receiving many forms of government transfer payments and transfers are reduced as earnings increase.

4 When losses of earnings due to various other government programs are balanced against income transfers, it is uncertain whether there are any net gains.

Historically, governments have subsidized many activities, including activities from which ethnic minorities were excluded or did not use for various reasons. The antebellum "free persons of color", for example, were taxed to support public schools from which their own children were excluded. Various Catholic ethnic groups have also been taxed for public schools which their children did not attend. While their lack of use of the public schools was voluntary, in some nineteenth-century schools the religious emphasis was so heavily Protestant that many Catholic parents felt that they had to educate their children elsewhere.

A wide variety of goods and services rarely used by low-income ethnic groups are subsidized by government out of taxes to which the latter contribute — recreational land use (state and national parks and forests), airport facilities, maritime subsidies, state universities, federal grants to higher education, tax shelters of many sorts, etc. On the other hand, a disproportionate share of welfare and public housing goes to low-income minorities. What is the net? *We do not know.* Different methods of computing it give different results. A revealing study of government money flowing in and out of a low-income black ghetto in Washington, D.C. showed that — despite huge welfare payments and expenditures on the public schools, as part of nearly $46 million of government spending there — there was an *outflow* of $50 million in taxes, so that this ghetto *lost* more than $4 million on net balance.[36] A cessation of all government transfers would have somewhat alleviated rather than aggravated their poverty.

The amount necessary to lift every man, woman, and child in America above the poverty line has been calculated, and it is *one-third* of what is in fact spent on poverty programs. Clearly, much of the transfer ends up in the pockets of highly paid administrators, consultants, and staff as well as higher income recipients of benefits from programs advertised as anti-poverty efforts.

In order to qualify for many government programs, one must be unemployed, earning below the official poverty level, or otherwise disadvantaged. This provides incentives to forego present earnings — and with it, forego human capital formation for the future. The government money currently received is not all net gain.

Finally, because minorities are, by definition, only part of a larger society, and many other groups with claims on government receive concessions whose economic impacts on minorities may offset all transfers put together. To make a very rough estimate of just one government activity, take the restrictive licensing of taxicabs. The number of taxis in Los Angeles is only one-fifteenth the number of taxis in Washington, D.C., even though Los Angeles is more than seven times the size of the nation's capital. If there were only five times as many taxis in Los Angeles as there are under restrictive licensing, that would mean thousands more jobs for which low-income minority members would be eligible instantly. When one considers that there are approximately 3,000 licensed occupations, the impact of this one government restriction looms very large.

There is no compelling reason to believe that government activity has benefitted ethnic minorities on net balance, even when that has been its purpose. The volatility of government policy suggests that determining its purpose over some meaningful span of time is also no easy task.

IMPLICATIONS

When the government chooses between policy A and policy B, it is making a choice in which the personal interests of the decision-maker are involved. Rewards for both elected and appointed officials — whether in money or in kind — come from increasing the demand for their services. If policy A will achieve a certain result largely through the individual efforts of the citizens themselves, and policy B requires the presence, activity, and visibility of politicians, clearly it is to the politicians' advantage to advocate policy B. It is also to the advantage of political organizations, individual "leaders", or various "movements" to favor the kinds of policies which promote their visibility and apparent importance.

Whatever the merits or demerits of particular government policies, nothing seems surer from history than that those policies will change. Within a period of twenty years, various state governments have permitted, prohibited, and then required racial and ethnic designations on employment records. Within the same span, the federal government has permitted, required, and then prohibited racially restrictive covenants in housing. The representation of minorities in the military and the civil service has undergone similarly extreme changes in a few decades. Questions about the role of government are not simply questions about whatever particular policies are being followed at a given time, but involve longer-run considerations about the effects of generating uncertainty about the ground rules within which individual plans and transactions can be made.

Epilogue

In the many kinds of economic transactions discussed in these chapters, we have been trying to understand emotionally charged social phenomena in cause-and-effect terms. Within that framework, we have been comparing the results under voluntary economic transactions ("the market") and when governmental action ("intervention") forces, penalizes, or subsidizes decisions different from those which the transactors would have preferred.

The many instances in which laws, regulations, and other governmental restrictions have produced economically detrimental results for various ethnic groups does not necessarily imply any special ineptness or depravity on the part of government officials. In many cases, the intention has been to benefit ethnic groups considered to need aid or protection. But even in those cases where the intention has been to thwart the advance of particular ethnic groups — the Chinese or Japanese, for example — these efforts have also largely failed.

Repeatedly ineffective or counterproductive actions — from minimum wage laws to housing regulations — suggest inherent limitations on what government can achieve. These have generally been limitations of knowledge rather than power. Even totalitarian states have had similarly counterproductive effects from their economic regulations.

The massive amounts of knowledge needed to coordinate a complex modern economy simply do not exist in any one place or with any small, manageable group of people. This knowledge consists not only of those standardized generalities known as "expertise", but also of innumerable particulars, including group capabilities, weaknesses, and aversions. Economists' convenient assumptions of homogeneous people without special traits or preferences are useful simplifications for many kinds of analyses. However, these postulates assume away the very particulars that define ethnicity.

Once having waved aside all differences between people, many social analysts are then left with no real explanation of intergroup differences in income, occupation, residential pattern, or other socio-economic outcomes. Only evil intentions — discrimination, racism, "exploitation" — are left as possible explanations. The general existence of sin among human beings virtualy insures that examples can always be found of bad behavior toward particular groups. The cause-and-effect question, however, is: to what extent are the various groups' economic conditions a function of others' sins? The presence of Jewish and Japanese Americans at the top of the income rankings must undermine any simplistic theory that discrimination is an overwhelming determinant of socio-economic position. It would be inexplicable how these groups could have higher incomes than Anglo-Saxons, despite a well documented record of anti-Semitism and anti-Oriental feelings, policies, and laws.

No two ethnic groups are identical in those variables which influence incomes or occupations. They differ by large amounts in age, education, regional distribution, and other factors. Moreover, a given group may differ greatly over time and at different places, and the rise (and sometimes fall) of groups is related to such changes over time in the group's own characteristics. The unrelenting struggle of the Catholic church to improve the behavior and values of the Irish and other nineteenth-century immigrants, [1] or the heroic efforts of the missionary teachers who went South after the Civil War to educate the newly freed blacks, [2] would be inexplicable if majority prejudices were all that mattered.

Economic analysis offers no way to make human beings morally better, kinder, or more tolerant toward those different from themselves. What it does offer is insight into the way different economic institutions affect the well-being of human beings as they are.

The central purpose of this book has not been its particular conclusions but the analytical approach — treating conflicting beliefs as empirically testable hypotheses, rather than as axioms or creeds.

Notes

Chapter 1: The Application of Economics

1 Charles Darwin, *The Origin of Species and the Descent of Man* (Modern Library).

2 Karl Marx and Friedrich Engels, *Basic Writings on Politics and Philosophy* (Doubleday Anchor Books, 1959), p. 399.

3 Data on the 1969 family incomes of Americans' of Japanese, Chinese, Filipino, West Indian, Puerto Rican, Black, and American Indian backgrounds were compiled from the 1970 Census Public Use Sample. These family incomes were then taken as a percentage of the national average family income generated by applying the same computer program specifications to the whole Public Use Samples as were used to generate the individual ethnic data. Data on 1969 family incomes of Americans of Polish, Italian, Irish, German, and Mexican ancestry were not directly available from the 1970 Census, but their 1968 and 1970 incomes were available from the U.S. Bureau of the Census, Current Population Reports ser. P–20, Nos. 213–21, 224, and 249, and an arithmetic average of the percentage that these two family incomes were of the national averages as reported in these respective publications was used as their percent of the national average family income. Data on the 1969 incomes of Jewish families are unavailable from the Census, because of constitutional limitations on government studies of religious groups. The data here were obtained from a private survey, the National Jewish Population Survey, compiled for the same year as the Census data.

4 US Bureau of the Census, *Social Indicators 1976* (Government Printing Office, 1977), pp. 454, 455.

5 Data for American Indians, Blacks, Chinese, and Japanese are from *US Census of Population, 1970, Subject Reports*, PC(2)

IF, IB, IG, respectively. Puerto Rican and Mexican data are from the Census Bureau's *Current Population Reports*, P-20, No. 213. All other group data are from *Current Population Reports*, P-20, No. 221, the "Russian" ancestry data in the latter being used as a proxy for Jewish.

6 See Thomas Sowell, "Ethnicity in a Changing America", *Daedalus*, vol. 107, No. 1 (Winter 1978), p. 221.

7 *Ibid.*, pp. 213, 218-220.

8 The ethnic data are from Thomas Sowell (ed.), *Essays and Data on American Ethnic Groups* (Urban Institute, 1978), pp. 260, 278. The general population data were tabulated from the same 1970 US Census, Public Use Sample, using the same computer program.

By the same definitions used in generating the ethnic data, the personal income by age bracket in the general population in 1969 was:

18-24:	$3,188
25-34:	$6,454
35-44:	$7,653
45-54:	$7,711
55-64:	$6,442
65+:	$3,208

9 *Ibid.*, p. 380.

10 US Bureau of the Census, *Current Population Reports*, P-20, No.224, p. 12.

11 US Bureau of the Census, *Historical Statistics of the United States: Colonial Times to 1970* (Government Printing Office, 1975), p. 297.

12 By 1967, black family income outside the South already exceeded the level reached by Puerto Rican family income in 1967. See US Bureau of the Census, *Current Population Reports*, P-23, No.46, p. 18 and P-20, No.213, p. 34.

13 US Bureau of the Census, *US Census of Population: Subject Reports*, PC (2) IF, pp. 158-163.

14 Sowell, "Ethnicity", p. 227.

15 See below, pp. 90–91.

16 Leo Grebler *et al.*, *The Mexican American People* (Free Press, 1970), p. 185.

17 *Ibid.*, pp. 18, 22-23, 250-253.

18 Sowell, "Ethnicity", p. 217. "Russian American" is the proxy for Jewish in this table.

19 Data for women of American Indian, Black, Puerto Rican, Filipino, Chinese, West Indian, and Japanese ancestry are

tabulated from the 1970 US Census Public Use Sample. See compilations in Sowell (ed.) *Essays and Data*, pp. 274, 292, 310, 328, 358, 394, 412. Other data are from the US Bureau of the Census, *Current Population Reports*, P-20, No.226.

20 US Bureau of the Census, *Current Population Reports*, P-20, No. 226, p. 20.

21 See Thomas Sowell, *Race and Economics* (David McKay, 1975) pp. 135-136.

Chapter 3: Job Markets

1 *Adam Smith, The Wealth of Nations* (Random House, 1937), p. 423.

2 Karl Marx and Friedrich Engels, *Basic Writings on Politics and Philosophy*, ed. Lewis S. Feuer (Doubleday Inc., 1959), p. 399.

Chapter 4: Consumer Markets

1 Oscar Handlin, *The Uprooted* (Grosset & Dunlap, 1951), p. 51.

2 Oliver MacDonagh, "The Irish Famine Emigration to the United States", *Perspectives in American History*, Vol. X (1976), p. 403.

3 Handlin, *The Uprooted*, p. 51.

4 MacDonagh, "The Irish Famine", p. 412.

5 Maldwyn Allen Jones, *American Immigration* (University Chicago Press, 1970), p. 1.

6 MacDonagh, "The Irish Famine", p. 394.

7 *Ibid.*, p. 395 n.

8 Abbot Emerson Smith, *Colonists in Bondage* (Peter Smith, 1965) pp. 3-4.

9 Jones, *American Immigration*, pp. 67-68.

10 Stephen Thernstrom, *The Other Bostonians* (Harvard University Press, 1973), p. 137.

11 Ivan H. Light, *Ethnic Enterprise in America* (University of California Press, 1972), p. 11.

12 Louis Wirth, *The Ghetto*, (University of Chicago Press, 1956) p. 229.

13 Light, *Ethnic Enterprise in America*, pp. 45-61.

14 See Nathan Glazer, *Affirmative Discrimination* (Basic Books, 1975), p. 154.

15 *Ibid.*, p. 155.

16 Thomas Sowell, *Race and Economics* (David McKay, 1975), p. 62.

17 David M. Katzman, *Before the Ghetto* (University of Illinois Press, 1975), p. 73.
18 Oscar Handlin, *Boston's Immigrants* (Atheneum, 1970), p. 114.
19 *Ibid.*, pp. 114-115. See also Jacob Riis, *How the Other Half Lives* (Harvard University Press, 1970), p. 9; Evan Maxwell, "Disease Control Dilemna", *Los Angeles Times* (23 July 1979), pp. lff.
20 St. Clair Drake and Horace B. Cayton, *Black Metropolis* (Harcourt, Brace and World, 1970), Vol. I. p. 176n. See also Allan H. Spear, *Black Chicago* (University of Chicago Press, 1967), chapter 1.
21 Katzman, *Before the Ghetto*, p. 26. See also pp. 55, 69, 73.
22 Gilbert Osofsky, *Harlem: The Making of a Ghetto* (Harper & Row, 1966), p. 12.
23 W. E. B. DuBois, *The Philadelphia Negro* (Schocken Books, 1967), pp. 7.
24 Constance M. Green, *The Secret City* (Princeton University Press, 1967), p. 127.
25 DuBois, *The Philadelphia Negro*, p. 326.
26 *Ibid.*, p. 306.
27 Jacob Riis, *How the Other Half Lives*, p. 99.
28 See Katzman, *Before the Ghetto*, pp. 35, 37, 102.
29 *Ibid.*, p. 160.
30 *Ibid.*, p. 138.
31 *Ibid.*, p. 139.
32 Drake and Cayton, *Black Metropolis*, Vol. I, pp. 44-45.
33 *Ibid.*
34 *Ibid.*, p. 45.
35 William Julius Wilson, *The Declining Significance of Race* (University of Chicago Press, 1978), p. 62.
36 Carter G. Woodson, *A Century of Negro Migration* (AMS Press, 1970), p. 82.
37 Thomas Sowell, "Three Black Histories", *American Ethnic Groups* (Urban Institute, 1978), p. 21.
38 Woodson, *A Century of Negro Migration*, pp. 82-83; Eugene Litwack, *North of Slavery* (University of Chicago Press, 1961), pp. 94-95.
39 Woodson, *A Century of Negro Migration*, p. 83.
40 James Weldon Johnson, *Black Manhattan*, p. 28.
41 Riis, *How the Other Half Lives* (Harvard University Press, 1970), p. 99.
42 DuBois, *The Philadelphia Negro*, p. 316.

43 Oscar Handlin, *The Newcomers* (Doubleday & Co., 1962), p. 47.

44 Robert Ernst, "The Economic Status of New York City Negroes, 1850-1863", *The Making of Black America*, ed. August Meier and Elliott Rudwick, (Atheneum, 1969), Vol. I, pp. 257-258; Richard Gambino, *Blood of My Blood* (Anchor Books, 1974), p. 76.

45 DuBois, *The Philadelphia Negro*, p. 33. See also pp. 34-35.

46 Osofsky, *Harlem*, pp. 43-44; Drake and Cayton, *Black Metropolis*, Vol. I, pp. 66-67, 73-76; Light, *Ethnic Enterprise*, p. 106; Woodson, *A Century of Negro Migration*, pp. 186-187; Spear, *Black Chicago*, p. 166.

47 E. Frazier, *The Negro in the United States* (MacMillan Co., 1957), pp. 281-285; Green, *The Secret City*, p. 207.

48 Woodson, *A Century of Negro Migration*, p. 180.

49 Riis, *How the Other Half Lives*, pp. 3, 4, 5.

50 Handlin, *The Newcomers*, p. 36.

51 Riis, *How the Other Half Lives*, pp. 13-14.

52 Robert Higgs, *Competition and Coercion* (Cambridge University Press, 1977), pp. 108-109.

53 Riis, *How the Other Half Lives*, pp. 80-81.

54 Jacob Rischin, *The Promised City* (Harvard University Press, 1967), p. 84.

55 Riis, *How the Other Half Lives*, p. 4, 4n. See also Francesco Cordasco (ed.), *Jacob Riis Revisited* (Doubleday, 1968).

56 Cordasco, *Jacob Riis*, p. 321.

57 *Ibid.*, pp. 349, 352.

58 *Ibid.*, pp. 348-349.

59 *Ibid.*, p. 351.

60 *Ibid.*, p. 350.

61 See Riis, *How the Other Half Lives, Passim.*

62 Irving Kristol, "The Negro Today is Like the Immigrant Yesterday", *New York Times Magazine* (1966, September 13).

63 Irving Howe, *World of Our Fathers* (Harcourt, Brace, Jovanovich, 1976), p. 148.

64 Theodore N. Ferdinand, "The Criminal Patterns of Boston since 1849," *American Journal of Sociology*, July 1967, p.87.

65 *cf.* J. C. Furnas, *The Americans* (G. F. Putnam's Sons, 1969), p. 701; *Report of the National Advisory Committee on Civil Disorders* (E. P. Dutton, 1968), p. 115.

66 Handlin, *The Uprooted*, p. 152.

67 Lawrence Friedman, *Government and Slum Housing* (Rand McNally, 1968), p. 30.

Chapter 5: The Economics of Slavery

1 John Hebron, "Simon Gray, Riverman: A Slave Who was Almost Free", *Mississippi Valley Historical Review* (December 1962), pp. 472-484.

2 William L. Westermann, *The Slave Systems of Greek and Roman Antiquity* (American Philosophical Society, 1955), pp. 13, 74, 79, 92, 110, 113.

3 J. C. Furnas, *The Americans: A Social History of the United States, 1587-1914* (G. P. Putnam's Sons, 1969), pp. 400-401.

4 Sowell (ed.), *Essays and Data on American-Ethnic Groups* (Urban Institute 1978), pp. 16-17.

5 *Ibid.*

6 Ulrich Bonnell Phillips, *American Negro Slavery* (Baton Rouge: Louisiana State University Press, 1969), p. 261.

7 Eugene D. Genovese, *Roll, Jordan, Roll* (Pantheon, 1974), p. 14.

8 Phillips, *American Negro Slavery*, p. 301.

9 Frederick Law Olmstead, *The Cotton Kingdom* (Random House, 1969), p. 215.

10 *Ibid.*, p. 70. See also U. B. Phillips, *Life and Labor in the Old South* (Little Brown and Co., 1953), p. 186.

11 Phillips, *American Negro Slavery*, pp. 301-302.

12 Phillips, *Life and Labor*, pp. 186-187.

13 Furnas, *The Americans*, p. 394.

14 Daniel Boorstin, *The Americans* (Random House, 1965), Vol. II, p. 101.

15 Phillips, *Life and Labor*, p. 186. See also U. B. Phillips, *The Slave Economy of the Old South* (Louisiana State University Press, 1968), p. 87.

16 Robert W. Fogel and Stanley L. Engerman, *Time on the Cross* (Little Brown and Co., 1974), pp. 109-117, 126.

17 Compare Genovese, *Roll, Jordan, Roll*, pp. 524-525 and Oliver McDonagh, "The Irish Famine Emigration to the United States", *Perspectives in American History*, Vol. X (1976), pp. 366-367.

18 Herbert S. Klein, *Slavery in the Americas* (University of Chicago Press, 1967), p. 188.

19 Olmstead, *Cotton Kingdom*, pp. 114-116.

20 *Ibid.*, pp. 119-120.

21 Richard C. Wade, *Slavery in the Cities* (David McKay, 1975), p. 110.

22 Westerman, *Slave Systems of Greek and Roman Antiquity*, p. 25.

23 *Ibid.*, pp. 59, 63, 65, 71.
24 *Ibid.*, p. 36.
25 *Ibid.*, p. 12.
26 *Ibid.*, p. 18.
27 Klein, *Slavery in the Americas*, pp. 257-258; Frank Tannenbaum, *Slave and Citizen* (Alfred A. Knopf, 1947), p. 100.
28 *Ibid.*, p. 18.
29 Mavis C. Campbell, "The Price of Freedom: On Forms of Manumission", *Revista/Review Interamericana* (Summer 1976), pp. 245, 250.
30 *Ibid.*, p. 246; Klein, *Slavery in the Americas*, p. 99.
31 Westerman, *Slave Systems of Greek and Roman Antiquity*, pp. 2, 9.
32 *Ibid.*, p. 63. See also p. 66.
33 Thomas Sowell, "Three Black Histories", *Essays and Data on American Ethnic Groups* (Urban Institute, 1978), p. 16; Clement Eaton, *The Freedom of Thought Struggle in the Old South* (Harper & Row, 1964), pp. 93ff., *passim*.
34 Harold B. Woodman, "The Profitability of Slavery: A Historical Perennial", *Journal of Southern History* (August 1963), pp. 303-325; Robert W. Fogel and Stanley L. Engerman, *Time on the Cross* (Little Brown and Co., 1974); Paul A. David *et al.*, *Reckoning with Slavery* (Oxford University Press, 1976).
35 Adam Smith, *The Wealth of Nations* (Random House, 1937), p. 365.
36 "Fortune never exerted more cruelly her empire over mankind, than when she subjected those nations of heroes to the refuse of the gaols of Europe". Adam Smith, *The Theory of Moral Sentiments* (Liberty Classics, 1976), p. 337.
37 See Thomas Sowell, *Classical Economics Reconsidered* (Princeton University Press, 1974), pp. 13-14.
38 For example, Phillips, *American Negro Slavery*, chapter XVIII.
39 See Fogel and Engerman, *Time on the Cross*.

Chapter 6: Government and Minorities

1 Irving Howe, *World of Our Fathers* (Harcourt, Brace, Jovanovich, 1976), pp. 540-541. See also *Abrams v. United States*, 250 US 616 (1919).
2 Ivan H. Light, *Ethnic Enterprise in America* (University of California Press, 1972), p. 174.

3 Mark R. Kramer and Michael S. Levy, *The Ethnic Factor* (Simon & Schuster, 1972), p. 61.

4 The Supreme Court ruled that Dred Scott, a slave, did not become free by being taken into a free territory, despite Congress' outlawing of slavery in the territory under the Missouri Compromise.

5 The Supreme Court ruled that "separate but equal" facilities were constitutional.

6 Jacob Riis, *How the Other Half Lives* (1970 edition), p. 3.

7 *Ibid.*, p. 21.

8 Walter E. Williams, "Government Sanctioned Restraints that Reduce Economic Opportunities for Minorities", *Policy Review* (Fall 1977), p. 23n.

9 Lorenzo J. Greene and Carter G. Woodson, *The Negro Wage Earner* (AMS Press, 1970), p.192.

10 Riis, *How the Other Half Lives*, p. 82.

11 *Ibid.*, p. 80.

12 *Ibid.*, p. 84.

13 Belton Fleischer, *The Economics of Delinquency* (Quadrangle Books, 1966), chapter 3.

14 Edward C. Banfield, *The Unheavenly City* (Little Brown & Co., 1970), p.150.

15 Thomas Sowell (ed.), *Essays and Data on American Ethnic Groups* (Urban Institute, 1978), pp. 11-17.

16 See Robert Higgs, *Competition and Coercion* (Cambridge University Press, 1977), p. 126.

17 *Ibid.*, p. 117.

18 See survey of the literature in James P. Smith and Finis Welch, *Race Differences in Earnings* (Rand Corporation, 1978), pp. 21-22. See also Thomas Sowell, *Affirmative Action Reconsidered* (American Enterprise Institute, 1975).

19 Stephen Birmingham, *Certain People* (Little Brown & Co., 1977), p. 186.

20 Charles L. Black, Jr., "Foreword: 'State Action', Equal Protection and California's Proposition 14", *Harvard Law Review*, Vol. 81, No. 69 (1967), p. 109.

21 Martin Mayer, *The Builders* (W.W. Norton & Co., Inc., 1978), pp. 24-25.

22 *Ibid.*, p. 25.

23 *Ibid.*, p. 206.

24 *Ibid.*, p. 208.

25 *Ibid.*

26 Birmingham, *Certain People*, p. 150; Thomas Sowell, "Led, and Misled", *New York Times* (1979, April 13), p. A27.

27 Wirth, *The Ghetto*, p. 255.
28 *Ibid.*, p. 256.
29 *Ibid.*, pp. 205, 207, 214, 215.
30 Humberto S. Nelli, "Italians in Urban America", *The Italian Experience in the United States*, ed. S. M. Tomasi and M. H. Engel (Center for Migration Studies, 1970), pp. 79, 91; William F. Whyte, *Street Corner Society* (University of Chicago Press, 1955), pp. xvi-xvii; Robert F. Foerster, *The Italian Emigration of Our Time* (Harvard University Press 1924), pp. 393-394.
31 Joseph Lopreato, *Italian Americans* (Random House, 1970), pp. 101-109.
32 Nelli, "Italians in Urban America", pp. 79, 97.
33 Nathan Glazer, *Affirmative Discrimination* (Basic Books, 1975), p. 154.
34 *Ibid.*, pp. 156-157.
35 Oscar Handlin, *The Newcomers*, pp. 13-15.
36 Murray N. Rothbard, *For a New Liberty: The Libertarian Manifesto* (Collier Books, 1978), p. 167.

Epilogue

1 Carl Wittke, *The Irish in American* (Russell & Russell, 1970), pp. 48-50, 92, 101, 145-146; Kathleen Neils Conzen, *Immigrant Milwaukee, 1836-1860* (Harvard University Press, 1976), pp. 159-164.
2 James M. McPherson, *The Abolitionist Legacy* (Princeton University Press, 1975), chapters 9-12.

Index